Chambers

Rude
Spanish

Chambers

CHAMBERS
An imprint of Chambers Harrap Publishers Ltd
7 Hopetoun Crescent, Edinburgh, EH7 4AY

Chambers Harrap is an Hachette UK company

© Chambers Harrap Publishers Ltd 2009

Chambers® is a registered trademark of Chambers Harrap Publishers Ltd

First published by Chambers Harrap Publishers Ltd 2009
Previously published as *Harrap's Rude Spanish* in 2004

Database right Chambers Harrap Publishers Ltd (makers)

A CIP catalogue record for this book is available from the British Library.

ISBN 978 0550 10549 3

10 9 8 7 6 5 4 3 2 1

www.chambers.co.uk

Designed by Chambers Harrap Publishers Ltd, Edinburgh
Typeset in Gill Sans by Chambers Harrap Publishers Ltd, Edinburgh
Printed and bound in Great Britain by Clays Ltd, St Ives plc

Contributors

Editor
Óscar Ramírez

Translations
Tim Gutteridge

"How to Swear in Spanish" author
Carmen Arnáiz

Illustrations
Glen McBeth

Publishing Manager
Patrick White

Prepress Controller
Clair Cameron

Trademarks

Words considered to be trademarks have been designated in this book by the symbol ®. However, no judgment is implied concerning the legal status of any trademark by virtue of the presence or absence of such a symbol.

Table of Contents

Introduction

*A*lthough slang or colloquial language, on the one hand, and rude or offensive language, on the other, tend to go hand in hand, they are certainly two different phenomena. One can frequently use colloquialisms to express oneself, and be perfectly polite, whereas someone else can express themselves in the Queen's English and sound terribly rude. The following pages combine examples which are merely colloquial with those of a truly offensive nature.

"¡Se sienten, coño!" is one of those phrases which remain ingrained in the collective Spanish memory. It was in this fashion that Lieutenant Colonel Tejero, standing gun in hand in the Spanish Parliament, asked the MPs to take a seat during the failed coup d'État back in 1981. This barely grammatical expression (it should have been "siéntense, coño") illustrates well how common swearing is in Spain. Whether to express surprise or strong views in an authoritarian way, it is a fact that Spaniards are more prone to swearing than Britons. That might be one of the reasons why swearwords do not have quite the same effect in Spain as they do in the United Kingdom, constant use having presumably watered down their strength.

In this respect, the translations provided in this alternative phrasebook, while preserving accuracy, aim at achieving as close an effect as possible to that in the ears of a native Spanish speaker, reflecting the nuances which usually go missing in a conventional bilingual dictionary. The reader will notice that, even in the rudest and most offensive Spanish examples, the c-word hasn't been used as a translation; this is not because of any sense of prudishness, but because it can be argued that none of the examples provided pack the same taboo punch as that notorious English word.

Although sometimes it is perfectly normal to pronounce a colloquial phrase in a standard fashion, certain expressions have to be pronounced in a more relaxed manner to sound natural (eg "estar pal arrastre" = "estar para el arrastre"). Therefore, when appropriate, the relaxed pronunciation is given in the Spanish example, followed by an explanation in brackets at the end.

Fifteen thematic chapters, complete with numerous examples, glossaries and humorous illustrations take up most of *Rude Spanish* . At the end of each chapter a "Test your rude Spanish" section will help you assess your knowledge of Spanish slang, and the solutions are provided at the end of the book. In addition to this, the book contains a section devoted to humour, with a handpicked selection of fully explained Spanish jokes and riddles, and a crash course on how to swear in Spanish.

The book also features an illustrated section on gestures which will help you understand some of the nuances of Spanish body language.

...rude accommodation

As you enter, your pupils dilate immediately, it's so dark. You advance peering into the gloom, hands feeling for the wall to support you. This might sound like the description of a very dark, spooky cave, but it's actually a pretty accurate picture of most Spanish flats. Indeed, every Spanish household boasts a complex system of blinds, shades and curtains to keep the sunlight out. And if you have a balcony the typical green awning is a must, although the more daring are breaking with tradition and opting for orange or even multicoloured patterns. We may want to let the light in, but keeping it out is in fact a necessity in most parts of Spain, particularly at the height of summer. If you have successfully found your flat and groped your way to the light switch, you are then ready to turn on the light and make the most out of this chapter.

A few useful phrases in context

Mis-selling

Le dijimos al de la agencia que queríamos pillarnos un hotel tranquilito con vistas al mar, y acabamos en un zulo con un ruidaco de obras insoportable

We told the guy at the travel agency we wanted a quiet little hotel with sea views, and we ended up in a dingy cupboard with a hellish racket from the builders

Nos cogimos aquel hotel porque el folleto publicitario decía que era muy céntrico. Y al final resulta que estaba en la quinta polla y que había que pillar tres autobuses para llegar

We booked the hotel because the leaflet said it was very central. But it turned out to be in the back of beyond and we had to catch three buses just to get there

Hotel sweet hotel

No pegamos ojo en toda la noche. Los de la habitación de al lado se pasaron todo el tiempo dándole al ñaca ñaca, y como las paredes eran de papel de fumar no nos perdimos ni un solo gemido

We didn't sleep a wink all night. The couple in the next room were at it all night, and because the walls were paper-thin we didn't miss a single grunt

La habitación parecía una convención de bichejos. Había de todo: moscas, cucarachas, gusanos y hasta algún que otro ratón. Y es que el cuartucho no había visto una fregona ni en pintura

The room was bug central. There was everything in there: flies, cockroaches, maggots and even a few mice. I don't think it had seen a mop since the hotel was built

1

RUDE ACCOMMODATION

Cuando le dijeron al recepcionista que había un zurullo flotando en la taza del váter, les soltó que como había sequía lo mejor era que tirasen de la cadena lo menos posible

When they told the receptionist there was a floater in the bog, he turned round and said that because of the drought it was best if they flushed the toilet as little as possible

Al abrir el grifo del agua caliente de la ducha me cayó un chorreón helado que me dejó tieso

When I turned on the hot water for the shower I got hit by a freezing jet that left me colder than a polar bear's bum

Nos pasamos todo el santo día pateando la ciudad y volvimos al hostal con los huesos molidos. Cuando nos metimos en el sobre nos dimos cuenta de que con la cantidad de muelles sueltos que tenía el colchón, ahí no iba a poder sobar ni un faquir

We spent the whole blasted day traipsing round the city and by the time we got back to the hostel we were absolutely knackered. But when we got into the sack we realized that the mattress had so many burst springs even a fakir couldn't sleep on it

meterse en el sobre

Tenants and landlords

Los inquilinos que tengo en mi piso se están columpiando que da gusto. Ya me deben tres meses de alquiler. Como no aflojen la mosca, la semana que viene los pongo en la puta calle

The tenants in my flat are really taking the piss. They already owe me three months rent. If they don't cough up, I'm going to kick them out on the bloody street next week

El dueño de mi piso es un jeta de mucho cuidado. Se presenta en el piso cuando le sale del forro. Le he dicho mil veces que antes de venir me dé un toque, pero no me hace mi puñetero caso

My landlord has got a real nerve. He turns up at the flat whenever he bloody well likes. I've told him a thousand times to call me before coming, but he doesn't take a blind bit of notice

With friends like these...

Dijo que se quedaría una semanita en mi casa hasta que encontrase piso. Lleva más de tres meses apalancado en el salón como Pedro por su casa y parece que la cosa va pa' largo

He said he'd kip at my place for a few days until he found a flat. He's been squatting in the living room for three months, and he's made himself so at home that it looks like he's here to stay

[pa' = para]

Paso de coger una habitación doble con María porque ronca como una condenada y, encima, es desordenada como ella sola

There's no way I'm taking a double room with María; she snores like a pig and is messy as hell

Your dream holiday

Se marcharon para una semana a una casa de campo para respirar aire puro. Pero tuvieron que volverse a los dos días porque no podían soportar el tufo de la mierda de las vacas y de las gallinas

They went off to spend a week in a cottage and breathe some fresh country air. But they had to come back after a couple of days because they couldn't stand the stink of cow dung and chickenshit

Glossary

bed: el catre, el sobre
dingy room: un cuartucho, un zulo
dirty: guarro
fall asleep (to): quedarse frito, quedarse sobado
in the middle of nowhere: en el quinto pino; *(stronger)* en la quinta polla, en el quinto coño
kick someone out (to): poner en la puta calle a alguien

noise: ruidaco
not sleep a wink (to): no pegar ojo
sleep (to): sobar
stay uninvited at someone's house (to): apalancarse en casa de alguien
toilet: el tigre, el meódromo, el meadero

Did you know...?

The word 'zulo' has a rather grim origin. It comes from Basque and it refers to the hiding place where ETA terrorists keep their kidnap victims or weapons. The word has recently made its way into colloquial Spanish with the sense of a pokey, dark room, often badly ventilated.

Test your rude Spanish

Try and match the Spanish sentence with its accurate English translation.

1. El albergue estaba en el quinto pino
a) The hostel was surrounded by pine trees
b) The hostel was in the middle of the countryside
c) The hostel was in the middle of nowhere

2. No pegamos ojo en toda la santa noche porque los vecinos tuvieron una bronca de aquí te espero
a) We didn't sleep a wink all night because the neighbours where having a nasty row
b) We got into a fight with the neighbours and I ended up with a black eye
c) The neighbour punched me and I got a black eye. I was so upset that I couldn't sleep a wink

3. Tenía los huesos molidos, me metí en el catre y me quedé frito en un santiamén
a) I was knackered. I got into bed and I fell asleep immediately
b) I was knackered. I got into bed and I couldn't sleep because of the fleas
c) I was knackered but hungry. I fried myself an egg before going to bed

...rude drinking

To the untrained eye, a 'bota' and a 'porrón' might seem two of the most peculiar objects to be found in Spain. They are actually two vessels for drinking wine: a leather bag with a nozzle (the 'bota') and a glass bottle with a spout (the 'porrón'), once described by George Orwell as "a dreadful thing resembling a bed bottle, especially when filled with white wine".

Do not expect to find them in trendy nightclubs, but rather in traditional restaurants or in 'tascas' — old and shabby-looking taverns with wooden tables and benches and a centuries-old accumulation of dirt, now pretty much on the verge of extinction, where local youths sing the weekend away or play at 'duro'. 'El duro' (the name for the old five-peseta coin) is a drinking contest, the aim of which is to get one of these coins into one of four glasses by bouncing it first on the table. It goes without saying that your chances of success diminish in proportion to the amount of alcohol you have imbibed. However, if you are planning to put some of the following into practice in any old tasca, our advice would be to handle the expressions with care, however emboldened by alcohol you may be.

A few useful phrases in context

How would you like it, sir?

Me da lo mismo que en esa disco den garrafón porque ya llevo un ciego que no me aguanto
I don't care if the booze they sell in that club is crap; I'm already so pissed I can hardly stand up

Cada día a las seis de la mañana, de camino al curro se para a fichar en el bareto de la esquina para meterse un lingotazo en el cuerpo. Dice que no hay nada como el carajillo de Veterano para recargar las pilas
Every morning at six o'clock on the dot he pops into the bar on the corner on his way to work to get a quick drink inside him. He says there's nothing like a coffee with a shot of brandy to recharge your batteries

Venga, vamos a hacer una ronda de coscorrones que parece que se está apagando la cosa
Come on, let's have a round of tequila slammers, it looks like things need livening up

Budget drinking

Han abierto un garito nuevo donde la priva está tirá
A new bar has just opened, and the booze is really dirt-cheap
[tirá = tirada]

5

Colega, me parece que vamos a tener que currarnos un simpa en este garito porque si no, nos vamos a quedar desplumaos en menos que canta un gallo

Looks like we're going to have to do a runner on the bill, if not, we're going to be skint as hell in no time at all

[desplumaos = desplumados]

Siempre están a dos velas. Cuando llega el viernes por la tarde van al súper a comprar cocacolas de tamaño familiar y vino peleón de cartón, y se curran unos calimochos que les duran todo el fin de semana

They're always completely skint. When Friday evening comes around they nip down to the supermarket for a few family-sized bottles of coke and some cheap plonk in cartons and mix them up; that keeps them going all weekend

vino peleón

Always in moderation

¡Arriba, abajo, al centro y pa'dentro!
Bottoms up!
[pa' = para]

Yo cuando cojo el puntillo paro de privar, porque si sigo, luego acabo haciendo el ridículo echando la pota encima de la chati que me quiero ligar cuando le estoy comiendo la oreja
Once I'm tipsy I stop drinking, because if I keep going I end up making an arse of myself and puking all over some girl I really fancy just when I'm in the middle of chatting her up

Nos pusimos a jugar al duro a saco: no paramos hasta que solo quedó uno de pie
We got into a serious drinking contest, and kept going until there was only one of us left standing

Este vinillo entra bien, pero sube un mogollón
This wine goes down easily, but it goes straight to your head

Siempre que voy de copas me llevo al chucho conmigo; así sé cómo volver a casa
When I go out for a few drinks I always take the mutt with me; that way, I know I'll be able to find my way home

It's going to hurt in the morning

Al ver la cola que había en el meódromo del bar y como llevaba una papa que no se aguantaba, Juan se fue al parque de delante a hacer un río. A la mañana siguiente se despertó de bruces en un parterre de rosas después de haber dormido la mona
Juan was as pissed as a fart so when he saw the queue in the bog he went to the park across the road for a slash. The next morning he woke up face down in a flower bed, having slept off the worst of it

Como llevaba un cebollón que no se tenía en pie, Manuel se tiró media hora tratando de meter la llave en la cerradura de su casa. Hasta que al ver que el vecino, cuchillo en ristre y cagado de miedo, abría la puerta desde dentro, se dio cuenta de que no era su casa
Manuel was pissed out of his skull and spent half an hour trying to get his key into the lock of his front door. It wasn't until he saw his neighbour opening the door from inside, knife at the ready and shitting himself with fear, that he realised that it wasn't his place

A Julián lo acababa de dejar la parienta y a Jorge le habían dao la patá en el curro. Así que se liaron a privar dale que te pego en un mano a mano. Los echaron del garito cuando se pusieron a cantar como almejas
Julián had just been chucked by his bird, and Jorge had got the sack, so they were doing some real heavy drinking. They got chucked out of the bar when they started singing like a pair of tom cats
[dao = dado; patá = patada]

7

Glossary

bar: un garito
beer: una birra
cheap booze: el garrafón, la priva de garrafa
coke and wine: un calimocho
do a runner (to): hacer un simpa
drink: la priva
drink (to): privar
drink a lot (to): empinar el codo, darle/pegarle a la botella
drunk (to be): ir ciego/mamado/pedo, llevar un cebollón
drunk (to get): coger un ciego/

un pedo/ un cebollón
drunkenness: el pedo
go out for a drink (to): ir de copas
rum or gin and coke: un cubata
scruffy bar: un antro (de mala muerte)
swig: un lingotazo
tequila slammer: un coscorrón
tipsy (to get): coger el puntillo
toilet: el tigre, el meódromo, el meadero

Did you know...?

A 'botellón', literally a 'big bottle', is a gathering at which groups of friends indulge in binge drinking, usually in a public park. Booze and snacks tend to be bought in supermarkets, making this an affordable way to get drunk. Neither the local community nor the police seem to find it a very amusing pastime.

Test your rude Spanish

Try and match the Spanish sentence with its accurate English translation.

I. Se pusieron hasta el culo con un vino peleón

a) They got into a fight after drinking some wine
b) They drank some wine and mooned at some tourists
c) They got drunk on some rough wine

2. Juan iba tan mamado que durmió la mona en el tigre del bareto

a) Juan was so drunk he fell asleep in the toilet of the bar
b) Juan got so drunk that he brought his monkey and tiger along to the bar
c) Juan got drunk while the monkey and the tiger slept

3. Se metió tres coscorrones en el cuerpo y cogió un pedo impresionante

a) He had three tequila slammers and started farting like there was no tomorrow
b) He was so plastered he didn't realize he was farting in front of everybody
c) He downed three tequila slammers and got plastered

...rude driving

When faced with the following question in their driving test:

Another driver does something that upsets you. What do you do?
a) try not to react
b) let them know in no uncertain terms how you feel
c) flash your headlights frantically several times
d) lean on the horn for several minutes

your Spanish would-be driver knows instinctively that the right answers can only be b), c) or d), accompanied by manic arm-waving whenever possible. But a little voice at the back of their head must tell them that if they want to keep their examiner happy and pass their test, they had better choose a). That surely is the only explanation for such discrepancies between theory and actual practice. And the truth is that in a country where pedestrian crossings are perceived as little more than an exotic touch in the urban landscape, each traffic light is seen as a new challenge and, luckily for us, an excuse for a colourful exchange of linguistic niceties.

A few useful phrases in context

Bad drivers

Ese no tiene ni puta idea de conducir. Se sacó el carné a la sexta
He's a bloody useless driver. He only passed his test at the sixth attempt

Bragging

Me piqué con un pardillo que como no dominaba acabó estampándose contra una farola
I had a race with this bozo, and he was such a crap driver he ended up crashing into a lamppost

Cada vez que me intentan pasar en una nacional, piso a fondo y me pego al que llevo delante, a mí no me adelanta ni Dios
Whenever anyone tries to get past me on an A-road, I put my foot down and stick tight to the guy in front. Nobody gets past me alive!

Me he comprado un carro nuevo alucinante, tronco, coge los 250
I've just bought a wicked new car, mate, it does over a ton fifty

Es un fantasma, le gusta salir de los semáforos quemando rueda
He's a real show-off. He always burns rubber when he moves away from the lights

"Hace un mes me metí un piño con el coche, di cinco vueltas de campana, y quedó siniestro total; yo no me hice ni un rasguño"
"Tú has visto muchas películas"
"A month ago I crashed the car; it rolled over five times and was a total write-off, but I walked away without a scratch"
"Yeah, right — and your real name is Michael Schumacher!"

Se cree que es el rey de la carretera, se salta todos los semáforos que le vienen en gana
He thinks the road belongs to him. He goes through red lights whenever he feels like it

Al llegar al semáforo apuró tanto la frenada que se llevó a una vieja por delante
When he came to the lights he slammed the anchors on so late that he flattened an old woman

Mira, esa se ha apalancado en el carril del medio, ha puesto el piloto automático y ya no hay quien la mueva; se cree que va sola
Look at that one sitting in the middle lane. She might as well be on cruise control — she won't budge for anyone. She seems to think the motorway's just for her

Technical problems

Menuda tartana que llevas, tía, es más lenta que el caballo del malo
What's that old crate you're driving? I've seen faster donkeys on Blackpool beach!
['caballo del malo' refers to the baddie's horse in Westerns, which tends to be very slow and seems never to catch up with the goodie's]

Tu coche es una verdadera cafetera, a ver si te lo cambias que ya toca
Your car's a real pile of junk. Don't you think it's about time you traded it in?

Cada fin de semana vienen los pijos de la ciudad con sus todoterrenos, se ponen a hacer caminos como locos y nos dejan el campo hecho una pena
Every weekend the toffs come down from the city in their 4x4s, off-road all over the place and leave the countryside looking like a dog's breakfast

Su nuevo buga zumbará todo lo que quiera, pero con lo que chupa de gasofa o le toca la lotería o solo lo va a poder sacar a dar un voltio una vez al mes
His new car may go like a bomb, but it gets through so much petrol that unless he wins the lottery he's only going to be able to take it out for a drive once a month

Easy riders

Salió del semáforo haciendo un caballito y su novia que iba de paquete acabó comiéndose el asfalto
He did a wheelie as he pulled away from the lights; his girlfriend was riding pillion and ended up with a mouthful of tarmac

hacer un caballito

Se pegó una tumbada con el pepino y se dejó media rodilla en la carretera
He leaned the bike over so far that he left half his knee behind on the road

Desde que me la truqué, colega, la burra tira que no veas
Since I souped up the engine, the bike goes like a bomb

Crime and punishment

Un pitufo me puso una receta por aparcar en doble fila
I got a ticket from a ticket warden for double parking

Se me llevó el coche la grúa y he tenido que apoquinar 200 euros del ala
My car got towed away and I had to cough up 200 euros

**Los pitufos me pararon la otra noche y me hicieron soplar; como iba un poco
mamado me quitaron el carné. Así que ahora me toca ir a pata a tos laos**
The traffic cops stopped me the other night and gave me a breath test, and I was
pissed so they took away my licence. Now I've got to schlep all over the place on
foot
[tos laos = todos lados]

I beg your pardon?

¿Te has sacado el carnet en una tómbola o qué? ¡Gilipollas!
Did you get your driving licence in a raffle, dickhead?

¡A ver si miras por dónde vas! ¡Mujer tenías que ser!
Look where you're going! Women drivers!

Oye, reina, los intermitentes los llevas para hacer bonito ¿o qué?
Hey, darling, do you think your indicators are just there for decoration?

¡Quita del medio, dominguero!
Get out of the way, Sunday driver!

¡La madre que te parió! ¡Que te has cruzado sin mirar, joder!
You bloody idiot! You just cut me up, for fuck's sake!

Misery

Qué mejor manera de acabar un fin de semana que encontrarse en un atasco al volver de la playa, el coche perdido de arena, 40 grados en la sombra y los niños berreando en el asiento de atrás: ¿estamos ya?
I can't think of a better way to round off the weekend than sitting in a traffic jam on the way back from the beach, the car lousy with sand, the thermometer at 40 degrees in the shade and the kids balling "are we there yet?" in the back seat

Me jode que cuando voy por la pista se me ponga uno detrás lamiéndome el culo
It really pisses me off having someone right up my arse when I'm on the motorway

Glossary

ace driver: el as del volante, el rey de la carretera
biker: un motero
breathalyze (to): hacer soplar
car: un carro, un buga
crash: un piño
crash into something (to): estamparse contra algo, pegársela contra algo, meterse un piño contra algo
fine, ticket: una receta
lean the bike over (to): hacer una tumbada/plegada, plegarse
motorbike: el pepino, la burra
motorway: la pista
old car: una cafetera

pillion passenger: el paquete
ride: un voltio
show-off: un fantasma
skilful driver (to be a): dominar
slow car: una tartana
step on the gas (to): meterle caña, pisar a fondo
Sunday driver: un dominguero
traffic policeman: un pitufo
two traffic police officers: la pareja (de la guardia civil)
use a lot of petrol: chupar mucha gasofa
very fast: a toda pastilla, a toda hostia

Did you know...?

In Spanish a 'smurf' is known as a 'pitufo'. Interestingly, the name of these affable little creatures takes on some rather offensive connotations when used as a slang term to refer to the Guardia Urbana (the traffic police in the cities). They are called 'pitufos' because they sport blue and white uniforms, just like the inhabitants of Smurfland.

Test your rude Spanish

Try and match the Spanish sentence with its accurate English translation.

I. Iba con su cafetera a todo lo que daba el motor y los pitufos le pararon y le hicieron soplar

a) He had a coffee to sober himself up because he knew the police might stop him for a breath test

b) He was speeding like mad in his old crate and the traffic cops stopped him to give him a breath test

c) The traffic cops stopped him to give him a breath test because he was driving very slowly in his old crate

2. Le encanta salir de los semáforos quemando rueda para asustar a los domingueros

a) He gets a thrill terrifying Sunday drivers by burning rubber when he pulls away from the lights

b) Last Sunday while waiting at the traffic lights his tyre burst and it gave him a fright

c) He hates Sunday drivers, particularly when they screech away from the lights

3. Dos burras nos adelantaron a toda pastilla por una nacional

a) Two mules overtook us while we were driving down a track

b) We saw two bikers speeding down the motorway like bullets. They must have been high on something

c) Two bikes overtook us at full throttle on an A-road

...rude food

'Pulpo a la gallega' (octopus, Galician style) is one of the most popular tapas dishes amongst Spaniards. The octopus has to be given a good beating against a chopping board or sink, preferably not whilst still alive, to soften up its flesh, and then is boiled until it is tender. Finally, it is well seasoned and served. If you are daring enough to have ordered octopus and happen to be eating one which is particularly chewy and rubbery, stop for a minute and look at the diners around you: Are they mostly speaking English? Are they wearing sandals and socks? Chances are you have ended up in a tourist trap and that the multi-legged animal you are eating has not been given the requisite bashing. The following examples might come in handy if you want to praise or make a complaint about someone's cooking skills, albeit in a rather unorthodox manner.

A few useful phrases in context

Rip-off

Por cuatro tapas de na' y un par de birras nos pegaron una clavada monumental; y encima no nos pusieron ni un triste chusco para mojar en la salsa
They charged us a bloody fortune for four measly tapas and a couple of beers, and they didn't even give us a miserable piece of bread to dip in the sauce
[na' = nada]

La cena en el restaurante de la otra noche nos costó un ojo de la cara. Pero mola mogollón porque das un chasquido con los dedos y tienes a todos los camareros lamiéndote el culo
Supper in the restaurant the other night cost us an arm and a leg. But it was really cool because all you had to do was click your fingers and you had all the waiters kissing your arse

Parasites and big eaters

Paso de invitar a cenar otra vez a los Alonso. Son unos gorrones natos. Se hinchan a papear y cuando llega la dolorosa siempre acabo yo haciendo de pagano
That's the last time I take the Alonsos out for a meal. They're natural born scroungers. They stuff themselves until they're fit to burst but when it comes to the hard part it's always muggins here who ends up footing the bill

Para quedar bien les saqué algo pa' picar a los Velasco, pero como comen como limas, tuve que acabar preparando una cena de tres platos y postre incluido
To be a good host I got some snacks out for the Velascos, but they eat like truck-drivers, so I ended up making them a three-course dinner with dessert to follow
[pa' = para]

Jaime papeando se queda solo. Cada día para merendar se pone hasta el culo; se mete unos bocatas de chorizo de dos metros

Jaime could eat for Spain. For his afternoon 'snack' he stuffs his face with a six-foot long chorizo sandwich

No me extraña que ya no le vayan los pantalones. Lo raro sería que le entrasen, porque con lo que se mete en ese cuerpo serrano le han salido unos flotadores de competición

I'm not surprised he can't squeeze into his trousers any more. It would be a shock if he could, what with all the food he puts away in that shapely body of his; he's got more spare tyres than the Michelin man

Decía que solo quería matar el gusanillo y en un plis-plas el muy buitre ha arramblado con todo lo que tenía en la nevera. Parece que tiene la solitaria, el muy cabrón

He said he just wanted a little something to keep his hunger at bay, and as quick as a flash the scrounging pig scoffed everything I had in the fridge. Anyone would think the bastard had a tapeworm!

matar el gusanillo

16

Not such a pleasure

Señora, este bistec será todo lo sabroso que Usted quiera, pero está más duro que la suela de un zapato. Como me acabe jodiendo el puente le voy a pasar la factura del dentista

Madam, maybe you're right that this steak is full of flavour, but it's also as tough as old boots. If I end up buggering my bridgework I'm going to send you the dentist's bill

Jo, tío, ten cuidado con ese bocata aceitoso que me estás dejando todo pringado

Hey, mate, careful with that greasy sandwich, you're getting me all covered with goo

Excellence?

Joder, macho, te has currao una cena que está para chuparse los dedos. Qué calladas te tenías tus dotes culinarias, cabroncete

Christ, mate, that dinner you cooked up was bloody delicious. You'd kept your culinary skills pretty quiet, you sly bugger

[currao = currado]

Todo el mundo pierde el culo con la cocina posmoderna de ese garito de Rosas. A mí, si quieres que te diga la verdad, que me deconstruyan una tortilla me la trae floja

Everyone's got their knickers in a twist about the post-modern cooking over at that gaff in Rosas. You want to know the truth? I don't give a toss for deconstructed omelettes

(Not so) Fresh produce

El pescadero decía que el besugo era de toda confianza. ¡No te jode, debía de ser como de la familia ya, porque por el tufo que echaba seguro que llevaba con ellos un par de mesecillos!

The fishmonger said he could recommend the bream. I bet he could give it a bloody character reference by now, because by the stink it was giving off I reckon he must've known it for a couple of months!

Este queso francés sabrá a gloria pero echa un tufo a podrido que no hay quien lo aguante

This French cheese may taste heavenly, but it stinks like hell

---

Glossary

baguette sandwich: un bocata
big appetite (to have a): tener la solitaria
bill: la dolorosa
charge someone a fortune (to): pegar una clavada a alguien
chips: las papas

delicious (to be): estar riquísimo, estar de rechupete, estar para chuparse los dedos
eat (to): papear, jalar, zampar
eat like a horse (to): comer como una lima
eat one's fill (to): ponerse las

botas, ponerse morado, ponerse hasta el culo, ponerse como el quico
fart: un cuesco
fat man: un tonel
fat woman: una vaca, una ballena, una foca
food: el papeo
greedy person: un zampabollos, un carpanta

keep one's hunger at bay (to): matar el gusanillo
person who pays the bill: un pagano, un paganini
rolls of fat on stomach: los michelines, los flotadores
scrounge a meal (to): comer de gorra
scrounger: gorrón, chupóptero

Did you know...?

In colloquial Spanish the word 'pagano' refers to 'the person who foots the bill' (from the verb 'pagar' meaning 'to pay'). It has a humorous touch to it because of its religious connotations in standard Spanish (it means 'pagan'). The variant 'paganini' is also used. Here the comic effect is achieved by adding the -i at the end, which gives it an Italian feel; in just the same way as in English we invent pseudo-Spanish words by adding an -o at the end.

Test your rude Spanish

Try and match the Spanish sentence with its accurate English translation.

I. Al ver la dolorosa por poco le da un patatús

a) He realized it hurt but he kept stuffing himself
b) When he saw the bill he nearly had a heart attack
c) It really hurt to have to pay so much for a few chips

2. Me voy a comer unas tapitas para matar el gusanillo porque llevo toda la santa mañana sin probar bocado

a) I'm going to have a few tapas to keep me going 'cause I haven't had a bite to eat all morning
b) I'm going to feed some tapas to my collection of worms 'cause they haven't eaten all morning
c) I'm going to have a few tapas 'cause killing that worm has left me exhausted

3. Se puso hasta el culo de alubias y se pasó la noche tirándose cuescos

a) She stuffed herself with beans and she spent the whole night farting
b) Her bottom was a bit sore because she had been sitting at the table all night
c) She stuffed herself with beans and she spent the whole night throwing up

...rude football

Contrary to popular belief, football and not bullfighting is the most popular spectacle amongst Spaniards. The country boasts four national daily sports newspapers, devoted almost exclusively to football, where rumourmongers will fill you in on the latest sexual scandal involving your favourite player. In addition, the sports section of the TV news takes up approximately one third of the programme, keeping the non-paper-reading part of the nation fully informed.

To enjoy a football match in a truly Spanish fashion, take a big bag of 'pipas' (sunflower seeds) along with you to the stadium. Eating them properly requires some specialist know-how, but with a bit of practice you should be able to achieve near-native competence, oblivious to the mess of empty shells you leave behind once the match is finished. Also, don't forget to take along your white handkerchief so that you can show either your disapproval or amazement at your side's performance by waving it in the air (you will have to follow the crowd on this one). Once you have memorized a few of the following phrases, you are ready to become a real aficionado.

A few useful phrases in context

The team

El Rayo ha vuelto a pinchar, a este paso van a Segunda de cabeza
Rayo have slipped up again; if they carry on like this they're going straight down to the Second Division

El Madrid le ha vuelto a meter una pana al Atlético
Real Madrid have thrashed Atletico again

Action

Hizo dos caños seguidos y le metió un trallazo a la bola que casi atraviesa la red
He nutmegged two players in a row and fired off a screamer that just about burst the net

Ha vuelto a hacer una filigrana de las suyas y ha dejao a toa la defensa plantá. Lo suyo es fútbol de dibujos animaos
He went on another one of his mazy runs and left the whole defence standing. This is real fantasy football
[dejao = dejado; toa = toda; plantá = plantada; animaos = animados]

Le hizo una segada al delantero del equipo contrario y el arbi lo mandó a la puta calle
He pulled down the opposition striker and the ref sent the bastard off for an early bath

19

hacer una segada

The players

Se han gastado un pastón en el fichaje de ese jugador extranjero, y la verdad es que es un verdadero paquete
They spent a packet on that new foreign player, but the truth is he's a real donkey

Este portero nuevo, además de tener manos de mantequilla, no ve ni una, ¡es un colador, el muy cabrón!
This new goalie's a real butterfingers, and he's as blind as a bat. The wanker couldn't stop a taxi!

En mi equipo no hay más que mantas, no mueven el culo ni a la de tres
All the players in my team are lazy as hell; they wouldn't run if their arses were on fire

La defensa la ha vuelto a cagar otra vez y han dejao al portero vendío. ¡Si es que no hay Dios que sude la camiseta!
The defence have screwed up again and left the goalie up shit creek. There's not one of them who's broken into a sweat
[dejao = dejado; vendío = vendido]

El nuevo delantero es un chupón acabado. No hay quien le haga soltar la bola y al final siempre le acaban robando la cartera
The new striker's really greedy. He hogs the ball like mad and he always ends up getting it taken off him

20

El central del Bilbao es un guarro de la hostia
Athletic Bilbao's centre half is dirty as hell

En el Barça no siente los colores ni el masajista. Eso sí, a final de mes bien que pasan por caja los muy buitres
None of the Barcelona team plays for the jersey. But when it comes to the end of the month the greedy sods are happy enough to collect their packet

Cuando lo fichó el Valencia, el petardo ese se creía que se iba a comer el mundo. Lleva cuatro meses en el club y no hace otra cosa que chupar banquillo.
When Valencia signed him, the prat thought he was on top of the world. He's been at the club for four months and he's spent the whole time sitting on the bench

The bastard in the black

El árbitro este es más casero que la madre que lo parió
This ref's a bloody homer!

¡Árbitro, estás cegato perdío! ¿No has visto que se la ha llevao con la mano?
You're blind as hell, ref! Didn't you see that he handled it?
[perdío = perdido; llevao = llevado]

¡Arbi, que te han dado el pito en una tómbola! ¡Si se ha tirado a la piscina, joder!
Ref! You must have got your whistle in a raffle! That was a blatant dive, for Christ's sake!

The football widow

¡Qué gracia tendrá ver a 20 energúmenos en calzoncillos corriendo detrás de un balón!
What fun watching 20 wallies in shorts running around after a ball!

Esta noche juega el Madrid, así que mi marido va hacer lo de siempre: apalancarse el mando a distancia y tragarse todo el partido
Real Madrid are playing tonight, so my husband will be up to his usual: he'll grab hold of the remote control and sit through the whole match

Glossary

Atlético de Madrid fan: un colchonero
bad goalkeeper (to be a): ser un colador
bad player: un paquete, un petardo
Barcelona fan: un culé
blind (to be): estar cegato, no ver tres en un burro
coach: el míster
dirty (to be): ser un guarro
dispossess (to): robar la cartera
fancy football: fútbol de dibujos animados, fútbol de otra galaxia
get a bad result (to): pinchar
greedy (to be): ser un chupón
hard shot: trallazo, pepinazo, cañonazo
lazy player: un manta
make a mistake (to): cagarla, hacer una cantada, hacer una cagada
nutmeg: un caño, un túnel
play dirty (to): jugar sucio/guarro
Real Madrid fan: un merengue
referee who favours home team: casero
scything tackle: una segada
sit on the bench (to): chupar banquillo
take a dive (to): tirarse a la piscina

Did you know...?

'Ser un colador', literally to 'be a colander', is a colloquial Spanish expression used to refer to a bad goalkeeper who concedes a lot of goals. The image is that of a goalie full of holes through which the ball can pass easily.

Test your rude Spanish

Try and match the Spanish sentence with its accurate English translation.

I. El nuevo fichaje es un verdadero paquete
a) They spent a packet on the new signing
b) They didn't spend much money on the new signing
c) The new signing is a real donkey

2. Han dejado al portero vendido y el delantero le coló un golazo sin despeinarse
a) The club sold the goalkeeper because he was a real butterfingers
b) They left the goalkeeper up shit creek and the attacker easily scored a great goal
c) The club has just signed a new goalie because the old one was a real butterfingers

3. ¡Menuda pandilla de mantas! Claro, cuando empiezan a ganar una millonada, los señoritos pasan de todo

a) What a shower of layabouts! When they start making big bucks, the snotty gits don't give a damn anymore

b) They really put their back into it. They earn every penny they get

c) The players have gone on strike because they say the pay is crap

The way in which some Brits do the washing-up is a source of amazement for Spanish people. Washing the plates and cutlery in the same bowl where, if at all, you might then rinse them will hardly earn you any points in a nation where the average household boasts two sinks — one for soaping and the other for rinsing.

Indeed, the Spanish take health and hygiene matters very seriously. They feel vindicated and take pride in the fact that their Mediterranean diet and their siestas, not that long ago perceived as food drowned in oil and a sign of laziness respectively, have been acclaimed and praised worldwide for their beneficial health properties. However, this obsession with well-being can be taken to an excessive degree. Take, for instance, the serious health hazard that walking shoeless (let alone barefoot) at home poses to your Juan Público. If you are bold enough to do this, grannies, mums and dads will all yell in unison: You're going to catch a cold!, and proceed immediately to fetch you a pair of slippers (actually, dads are not very likely to lift a finger). To be fair to these concerned, Spanish floors are often covered in tiles of an unusually refrigerated quality. Likewise, your Spaniard does not get rained on, full stop. Cases of people rushing into the cinema they have just walked past to avoid a sudden downpour are not unheard of. Better to sit through two hours of a cheesy American blockbuster than to catch a cold or, even worse, pneumonia, is the logic.

Although your health is very likely to be well looked after in Spain, the following provides a number of ways to express your complaints if you are in a rather feisty mood.

A few useful phrases in context

Symptoms

Cariño, cada vez que escupes sueltas unos lapos negros recubiertos de coágulos de sangre. ¿Seguro que es normal?
Darling, every time you spit you bring up great black lumps of snot covered in blood. Are you sure it's normal?

Desde hace un mes me duele la espalda una barbaridad. Pero paso de ir al matasanos, porque cada vez que entro un ambulatorio me cago por la pata abajo
My back's been hurting like hell for a month. But there's no way I'm going to see a quack. Whenever I go to the doctor's I get the heebie-jeebies

Not so caring docs

Le tocó un carnicero de cirujano, y para una triste operación de apendicitis la han dejado hecha un Cristo

She ended up with a real butcher of a surgeon; she was only having her appendix out but they made a right dog's dinner of it

Doctor, a ver si acierta ya con la puñetera aguja porque me está dejando el brazo hecho un colador

Doctor, do you think you could manage to find the right spot for that bloody needle? My arm isn't a pincushion!

What's up doc?

Señor Benítez, es la tercera vez que viene a la consulta para que le mire ese bultito. Es usted un pupas. Ya le he dicho que eso no es nada, que es una chorrada. Está usted como un toro

Mr Benítez, this is the third time you've come along to the surgery asking me to look at that lump. You're a moaning minnie. I've told you there's absolutely nothing wrong. You're as fit as a fiddle

Los manchurrones que le han salido a su hijo no son nada grave. Son eso: manchurrones. Coja jabón y una esponja y lave al niño de una vez que ya le toca y canta que da gusto

The blotches which have just appeared on your son aren't anything serious. In fact, blotches is all they are. Take some soap and a sponge and give the lad a good wash; it's about time, he stinks to high heaven

Tiene usted que dejar de beber, señor Gumersindo, porque se está castigando el hígado de mala manera y se lo está dejando hecho paté

You've got to stop drinking, Mr Gumersindo; if you carry on punishing your liver like this it's going to end up like a football

Se jodió la espalda y el matasanos le recetó reposo absoluto durante un mes. Pero como es un salido, al día siguiente ya estaba dándole que te pego con la vecina del quinto

He buggered his back and the doc told him he had to rest it completely for a month. But he's such a randy sod that the next day he was at it with the woman from the fifth floor

Mental health

Desde que lo dejó la novia parece que no carbura bien. Se pasa el día tumbado en el sofá tragándose todos los programas basura que echan por la tele

Since his girlfriend left him it looks like his brain's packed in. He spends the whole day lying on the sofa watching any old garbage that's on the telly

Tiene una depre de caballo encima desde que lo echaron del curro. Le he dicho que fuéramos a echar una canita al aire, pero ni con esas, no hay nada que hacer

He's been really down since he got the sack. I told him he should get his leg over but I was wasting my breath, he's a hopeless case

Health hazards

¿Que se te han dormido los pies, dices? En vista de lo que cantan, esos quesos están muertos, no dormidos

What's that, your feet have gone to sleep? Are you sure that's all they've done? It smells more like there are a couple of corpses decomposing in your shoes

Bad luck!

Nunca se había puesto enfermo, no le dolía nada. Y un buen día, coge un triste resfriado y la palma

He'd never been ill or even had any aches and pains. Then one day he catches a stupid cold and goes and snuffs it

Prognosis: positive

Los médicos le habían dicho que ya estaba pal arrastre y que no duraría más de un mes. Han pasado cinco años y ella está más fresca que una rosa

The doctors told her that she was on her last legs and would be dead within a month. That was five years ago, and she's still in great nick

[pal = para el]

estar más fresco que una rosa

Maternity

La Pili se puso de parto y al bebé ya le asomaba medio tarro; cuando llamó al hospital, le dijeron que aguantara porque no les quedaban catres libres
Pili went into labour and the baby's bonce was already half sticking out; when she called the hospital they told her to hang on because there weren't any empty beds

A mi mujer se le han puesto los cántaros como dos globos, y tiene complejo de vaca lechera. Dice que ya no da más teta, que si el bebé tiene hambre que tome potitos
My wife's tits have swollen up like two watermelons, and she feels like a dairy cow. She says that she's had it with breastfeeding — if the baby's hungry he can have some babyfood

Glossary

armpit: el alerón
bad surgeon: un carnicero
bottom: el culo, el pompis, el pandero
breasts: las tetas, los cántaros, el tetamen, las domingas
crazy (to be): estar gagá
depression: una depre
die (to): palmarla, diñarla
doctor: un matasanos
face: el careto, la jeta
fingers: los dátiles
fit: un patatús
foot: el queso, la pezuña
hand: la zarpa
head: el tarro, la perola, el coco
hypochondriac (to be a): ser un pupas
leg: la pata
mental hospital: un loquero
nose: la napia
penis: la polla, la picha, el rabo, la minga, el cipote

punish one's liver (to): castigarse el hígado
scared (to be): estar cagado, cagarse por la pata abajo
smell bad (to): cantar, echar/pegar tufo
smoke a lot (to): fumar como un carretero
spit: un lapo
teeth: los piños
testicles: los cojones, los huevos, las pelotas
tired (to be): estar roto/molido/muerto/hecho polvo
tongue: la sin hueso
vagina: la almeja, el conejo, el chocho
very bad health (to have): estar para el arrastre
very good health (to have): estar como un toro, estar como una rosa

Did you know...?

Quite a few bullfighting terms and expressions have made their way into everyday Spanish usage. The expression 'estar pa'l arrastre' ('estar para el arrastre' in its full form) is a good example. It means 'to be on one's last legs', although the original phrase refers to the dead bull which is ready to be dragged out of the ring by a team of mules.

Test your rude Spanish

Try and match the Spanish sentence with its accurate English translation.

I. Esos quesos echan un tufo a podrido insoportable. Se me está revolviendo el estómago

a) That cheese stinks like hell. I'm sure that's why I have such a bad tummy

b) That cheese has a rather pungent smell to it; it is delicious though

c) Those feet stink like hell. They're making my stomach turn

2. Fumaba como un carretero. Cogió un cáncer de pulmón y la palmó

a) He used to smoke like a chimney. He got lung cancer and he snuffed it

b) He used to smoke like a chimney. But he didn't want to get lung cancer and he gave up

c) He was a light smoker. Even so he snuffed it from lung cancer

3. Le salió un bulto en la perola y se cagó por la pata abajo. El matasanos le dijo que era una chorrada

a) He noticed a lump on his head and he got dead scared. The quack told him it was nothing to worry about

b) He noticed a lump on his nose and he got dead scared. The quack told him they would have to carry out some tests

c) He noticed a lump on his bottom when he went to the loo. The quack told him it wasn't looking great

...rude nationalities

NB: Readers are advised that this section contains some expressions of a racist nature

Twenty or so years ago, your average Spanish family could not afford to go abroad on holidays. Things have changed quite a lot but nevertheless most Spaniards choose to holiday within Spain. They certainly love their homeland and are proud of it. To some extent, such passion for their country was instilled back when the national TV channel, little more than a mouthpiece for Franco's propaganda machine, constantly reminded them what a glorious country Spain was, almost a paradise on Earth. The attitude towards foreigners then was something like: 'they may have the cash, but this is the place to be'.

Of course, the sun-drenched paradise that is Spain is not as homogeneous a nation as it might seem at first sight, and each region has its own distinctive customs and character. For instance, Andalusians are notoriously workshy, people from Aragon rather stubborn, Castilians too serious for their own good, Catalans stingy, and Galicians superstitious. And everybody knows that people from Madrid (madrileños) are big show-offs. A trifle judgmental? Not really, this was the result of a survey organized by the Centro de Investigaciones Sociológicas (a body which conducts sociological surveys for the Spanish Government) on how Spaniards see each other! Below you will find how to express these and other prejudices in rather robust language.

A few useful phrases in context

What are they like!

Los gabachos, cada vez que les da la vena, se bajan a la frontera y nos queman los camiones de frutas porque nuestras exportaciones son demasiado baratas, y la policía franchute ni puto caso. ¡A la legión tendríamos que enviar para que se enterasen de lo que vale un peine!

Whenever the frogs feel like it they close the border and start burning our fruit lorries because our exports are too cheap, and the French police don't lift a bloody finger. We ought to send the paras in to teach them some sense!

Los cabezas cuadradas cada año invaden Mallorca. Es como la época del expansionismo pero a lo guarro, porque nos dejan todas las playas perdidas de mierda

Every year the krauts invade Majorca. It's like a filthy rerun of World War Two, because they leave the beaches covered in crap

De tos los sudacas que vienen a España los porteños son los más espabilaos. Se montan un negociete de psicología para dar consejos a cuatro pringaos y, hala, a forrarse

Of all the Latin Americans who come to Spain, the ones from Buenos Aires have got it sussed. They set themselves up as shrinks, find four dickheads to analyse and before you know it they're rolling in cash

[tos = todos; espabilaos = espabilados; pringaos = pringados]

Cuatro pobres moracos llegaron la semana pasada en patera a Tarifa. De comité de recepción se encontraron a grupo de skinheads que los pusieron a caldo con porras y cadenas

Four towelheads made it to Tarifa in a dinghy last week. The reception committee was a group of skinheads who beat the crap out of them with truncheons and chains

Regional Spanish stereotypes

Vosotros los andaluces tendréis mucho salero, pero de currar, poquito, majete. ¡Si os pasáis el día de juerga o haciendo la siesta a la sombra de un olivo! Y encima a final de mes os cae el PER a tocateja

You Andalucians are a right bunch of jokers, but you're not so keen on a bit of hard work. You spend the whole day having a good time or sleeping your siesta under an olive tree. And then come the end of the month you pocket your rural unemployment benefit

Los polacos encima de agarrados son unos buitres del copón. Cada dos por tres vienen a Madrid a mendigar más pasta. Y encima hay que tragar mecha con el rollo del idioma. ¡Que hablen en cristiano y se acabaron los problemas!

The Catalans are not just as tight as a nun's chuff, they're also a bunch of bloody scroungers. They never stop begging money off the central government in Madrid. And then we have to put up with all that guff about their language. If they could talk properly we wouldn't have all these problems!

Mira, Juan, los castellanos seréis todo lo nobles que tú quieras, macho. Pero tenéis la gracia en el culo

Look, Juan, you Castilians may well be honest as hell. But you're all about as funny as a nosebleed

Tengo un amigo maño que a cabezón se queda solo. Se le metió en la cabeza que no quería que su chati llevase falda. Como le taladró tanto la olla, la pava ha acabado poniéndose pantalón para no oírlo

I've got a friend from Aragon who's as stubborn as hell. He got it into his head that he didn't want his bird to wear a skirt. He banged on at her about it so much that she ended up wearing trousers to shut him up

Cada verano las costas de Valencia se nos llenan de chuloplayas madrileños

Every summer the beaches around Valencia fill up with macho posers from Madrid

Estos vascos son más brutos que un arao. Para matar el rato primero se lían a cortar troncos con un hacha y después se ponen a levantar esos mazacotes de piedra pesadísimos. De verdad que parecen masocas

These Basques are real meatheads. Their idea of fun is to chop up logs with an axe and then lift up some bloody great boulders. Anyone would think they were into SM

[arao = arado]

A few idioms using nationalities

Literal meanings are followed by the actual translations.

Hacer el indio
to play the Indian
to play the fool

Engañar a alguien como a un chino
to cheat someone as if they were a Chinaman
to take someone for a ride

33

RUDE NATIONALITIES

Hacerse el sueco
to pretend to be Swedish
to act dumb

Despedirse a la francesa
to say goodby 'à la française'
to leave without saying goodbye

Beber como un cosaco
to drink like a Cossack
to drink like a fish

Trabajar como un chino
to work like a Chinaman
to work one's arse off

Ser más tonto que un chino
to be more stupid than a Chinaman
to be as thick as two short planks

Trabajar como un negro
to work like a black man
to work one's arse off

Ser un cuento chino
to be a Chinese tale
to be a cock-and-bull story

Glossary

black person: un negraco
Catalan: un polaco, un catalufo, un catalino
conman: un gitano
foreigner: un guiri
French person: un gabacho, un franchute
German: un cabeza cuadrada
immigrant to Basque Country from elsewhere in Spain: un maqueto
immigrant to Catalonia from elsewhere in Spain: un charnego
North African: un moro, un moraco
South American: un sudaca

Did you know...?

You usually say to someone 'háblame en cristiano' (literally 'talk to me in Christian') when you want the person in question to talk to you in a language you understand, whether literally (ie Spanish) or because they are talking gibberish. In either case, the expression tends to have pejorative connotations.

Test your rude Spanish

Try and match the Spanish sentence with its accurate English translation.

I. Los cabezas cuadradas se despidieron a la francesa

a) The frogs are as stubborn as the krauts

b) The frogs left without saying goodbye

c) The krauts left without saying goodbye

2. Los polacos son todos unos ratas de aquí te espero. Y encima se empeñan en no hablar cristiano

a) Poles are stingy as hell. On top of that they refuse to speak properly

b) Basques are stingy as hell. On top of that they are a bunch of blasphemous infidels

c) Catalans are stingy as hell. On top of that they refuse to speak properly

3. Ese es un gitano de mucho cuidado. Siempre trata de darte gato por liebre

a) He is a crafty devil. He's always trying to cheat you

b) Gypsies love animals, particularly cats and hares

c) He is a crafty devil. He cheated a gypsy the other day

...rude nightclubbing

For most Spaniards, not meeting up with your clubbing friends until around midnight on Friday or Saturday (or any other day of the week, for that matter) sounds like a very sensible option. To give yourselves a bit of Iberian courage, a good couple of hours are spent crawling from bar to bar making the most of the affordable drinks, before the overpriced nightclub booze. At around 2 am, your previously deserted club starts to get lively and the place is usually swarming with people by 3 am; which, of course, makes this the time you are most likely to find yourself a partner. Unsuccessful suitors, however, can always take solace afterwards in the well-established Spanish comfort food: 'chocolate con churros' (thick hot chocolate with 'churros' – a type of doughnut), which will certainly help to sober you up.

A few useful sentences in context

Warming up

Esta noche voy de caza a saco, le voy a entrar a todo el que se me ponga a tiro
I'm going out on the pull tonight, I'm going to chat up any bloke who comes within shouting distance

Me ha dicho Pedro que presiente que esta noche moja, y yo le he contestado que con ese careto de simio no se va a comer un rosco
Pedro told me he's got a feeling he's going to get his leg over tonight, but I said that with his ugly mug he's never going to pull

Esta noche pasamos de ir al Pato Mareado porque chapan pronto y, además, ahí entiende hasta el apuntador
Let's not bother going to the Dizzy Duck tonight. It closes early and it's as gay as it can get; even the bouncers are queens

Action

En esa disco ayer me clavaron 25 euros del ala por la entrada
They stung me for 25 euros just to get into that club last night

No veas, colega, qué polvo que tiene la tía esa
Christ's sake, mate: I wouldn't mind shagging her!

"Hay dos niñas que me hacen tilín y no sé a cuál tirarle los tejos"
"No te lo pienses, tío, ante la duda, la más tetuda"
"There are two girls I really fancy, and I don't know which one to go for"
"Don't think twice about it: when in doubt, big tits get my shout"

Voy a entrarle a ese macizorro
I'm going to chat up that gorgeous hunk

Ma pillao un pavo por banda y ma pegao un morreo que casi me asfixia. Y le he soltao un rodillazo en los huevos que sa quedao a gusto
This jerk got his paws on me and stuck his tongue so far down my throat I could hardly breathe. I sorted him out with a knee in the bollocks
[ma pillao = me ha pillado; ma pegao = me ha pegado; sa quedao = se ha quedado]

No veas cómo está el ganao en este garito, tío
The talent isn't half bad in this bar, mate
[ganao = ganado]

A este tío siempre le pasa lo mismo, al principio todas las tías le parecen unos cardos pero al final de la noche baja el listón y se lo acaba montando con la más foca
It's always the same story with him. At the beginning of the evening he thinks all the girls are dogs, but by the end of the night he's lowered his standards and ends up getting off with any old whale

ser una foca

Estoy hasta el moño de ese baboso. Lleva toda la noche pegado a mí como una lapa y no me lo quito de encima ni a la de tres

I'm sick to death of that lech. He's spent the whole night stuck to me like a piece of chewing gum, and I can't get shot of him

Yo paso de nadadoras, a mí me van las chatis con dos buenas peras

I don't go for girls with chests like ironing-boards. I like chicks with big jugs

Drugs

Hey, quédate, he pillado material del bueno; esta noche nos vamos a poner hasta el culo

Hang around, I've scored some fab gear; we're going to get really stoned tonight

Paso de enrollarme con el drogata ese que se mete de todo: se chuta, esnifa y fuma por un tubo

There's no way I'm getting off with that druggie. He takes anything he can get his hands on: he shoots up, snorts and smokes like there was no tomorrow

He ido al tigre a hacerme un peta, han venido dos seguratas y me han ligado toda la mierda que llevaba

I went to the bog to roll a joint, and a couple of bouncers came and took all my dope off me

Ma dao un bajón y estoy que no me aguanto

I'm having a whitey and I can hardly stand up

[ma dao = me ha dado]

Este costo pone un mogollón

This hash is really strong shit

Esta noche he empalmao, me voy a meter algo para animarme porque si no, me sobo

I've just pulled an all-nighter. I'm going to take something to give me a lift, otherwise I'm going to crash out

[empalmao = empalmado]

Disappointment

Cuando se tomó el quinto cubata a Juan se le fue la olla y comenzó a magrear a una chati. Los seguratas lo sacaron de la disco a guantazo limpio

After his fifth rum and coke, Juan completely lost it and started trying to feel up this bird. The bouncers kicked him right out of the club

Pedro va pasao de vueltas. Fijo que acaba en el tigre echando la pota

Pedro's pissed out of his head. I bet he ends up puking his guts up in the bog

[pasao = pasado]

Manuel iba de guays toda la noche, se pensaba que mojaría. Le ha tirao los tejos a mogollón de chatis, y al final no se ha comío un rosco

Manuel was shooting his mouth off all night, thinking he was going to get laid. But he tried to chat up loads of birds and he didn't even come close to pulling

[tirao = tirado; comío = comido]

Yo me abro, pavo, porque la peña de aquí son unos muermos. Hay menos marcha que en un velatorio

I'm off, mate, this crowd's boring as hell. You'd get more action at a wake

No se comió un rosco en toda la noche, y acabó a las 9 de la mañana más solo que la una, comiendo churros para que se le pasase la mona

He didn't get off with anyone all night, and ended up all alone at 9 in the morning, trying to sober up with a bag of churros

Glossary

alcohol: la priva
attractive man: un tío bueno, un macizorro
attractive woman: una tía buena, una jaca
bar: un garito
boaster (to be a): ir de guays
bouncer: el segurata
boy, man: un pavo, un maromo, un tío
breasts: las tetas, las peras
buy drugs (to): pillar
cannabis: el costo, el chocolate, la mierda
cheap (to be): estar tirado
close (to): chapar
cocaine: la coca, la farlopa, la nieve
drug addict: un drogata
ecstasy: una pasti
excite sexually (to): poner
fail to find a partner (to): no comerse un rosco
fall asleep (to): sobarse
flat-chested woman: una nadadora, una tabla de planchar
fondle (to): magrear, sobar, meter mano
gay (to be): entender
girl, woman: una pava, una chati, una niña
give a high (to): poner, colocar
go out on the town (to): ir de juerga/farra/fiesta
great looks (to have): estar como un tren, estar muy bueno, estar macizo, estar como para

mojar pan, *(stronger)* tener un polvo
group of friends: la peña
heroin: el jaco, el caballo
high (to be): ir puesto, ir colocado
high (to get): colocarse
inject drugs (to): chutarse, picarse
kiss passionately (to): morrear
leave (to): pirase, abrirse
lecher: un baboso
look for a partner: ir de caza
lower one's standards (to): bajar el listón
make advances to (to): tirarle los tejos a, entrarle a
marijuana cigarette: un porro, un canuto, un peta, un petardo
overweight unattractive woman: una foca
pair off with (to): enrollarse con, montárselo con
people: la peña
pick up (to): ligarse a
potential partners: el ganado
scruffy bar: un antro (de mala muerte)
sex (to have): mojar
sick (to be): potar, echar la pota
sleep all night (not to): empalmar
state of intoxication: el colocón
tab of LSD: un tripi, una pirula
toilet: el tigre
unattractive person: un cardo, un engendro

Did you know...?

Spaniards do not seem to appreciate the beauty of the thistle quite as much as they do, say, in Scotland. Indeed, 'cardo' (thistle) or even worse 'cardo borriquero' (cotton thistle) are used to refer to a person with unfortunate looks. Hence, 'ese tío es un cardo borriquero' could be faithfully rendered as 'that bloke's as ugly as sin'.

Test your rude Spanish

Try and match the Spanish sentence with its accurate English translation.

1. La pava esa está como para mojar pan

a) That girl's gorgeous
b) That girl's high on something
c) That girl eats like a pig

2. Esta noche fijo que mojo

a) I bet you I get lucky tonight
b) I bet you I get high tonight
c) I bet you I get plastered tonight

3. No vayas a ese garito porque te clavan

a) Don't go to that bar because someone got stabbed there last week
b) Don't go to that bar because there are hardly any girls
c) Don't go to that bar because the prices are very steep

...rude officialdom

Back in 1833, Mariano José de Larra, a prominent Spanish journalist and writer, published a well-known article entitled: "Vuelva Usted mañana" (Come Back Tomorrow). It tells the story of Sans-délai, a fictitious French gentleman who goes to Spain to sort out some family legal matters and to invest a sizable sum of money. Thinking initially that it would take him a fortnight at the most to finalize these formalities, he actually doesn't leave Spain until six months later, frustrated that he has made no progress at all since first setting foot in the country. It seems that back then tomorrow never arrived and when it did you were very likely to have your application turned down anyway. Although nowadays Spanish private businesses seem to be pretty much on a par with their European counterparts in terms of speed and efficiency, government agencies remain true to the 'mañana' doctrine.

Interestingly enough, 'los funcionarios' (public sector workers) still top the charts as Spain's most desirable occupation, and they are widely seen as a job for life in which the workload is allegedly non-existent. If you find yourself in the situation of having to deal with any branch of Spanish bureaucracy, make sure you take a good book with you and plenty of patience; alternatively, practise your Spanish small talk and learn a few of the following examples so that you can share your views with your fellow queuers.

A few useful phrases in context

Speed and efficiency

El de la ventanilla se puso borde y le dije que escribiría una carta de reclamación. Aunque se la pasarán por el forro, como de costumbre

The guy at the window got lippy so I told him I was going to write a letter of complaint. Although they'll only chuck it straight in the bin, as always

Tres horas haciendo cola y ahora me dicen que me falta no sé qué impreso de mierda. Ya son ganas de tocar los cojones

Three hours standing in a queue and now they tell me that Christ-knows-what bloody form is missing. They love to piss you off

No me sale de los huevos ir a hacer cola pa' renovarme el DNI. Que se lo metan por el culo. Y la próxima vez que me pida el carné la poli, que se me lleven palante si quieren

I can't be shagged queuing up to renew my ID card. They can stick it up their arses. And the next time the cops ask to see my card they'll just have to drag me down to the station

[pa' = para; palante = para adelante]

43

"Alucino en colores. Hace un mes eché los papeles para pedir un subvención. Me la dieron en una semana"

"¿Seguro que no lo has soñado?"

"I was gobsmacked! A month ago I sent off the forms to apply for a grant, and they gave it to me within a week"

"Are you sure it's not a dream you had?"

Primero vete a no sé dónde a buscar un papel. Luego vente paquí a que te lo sellen. Després entrégalo en no sé qué oficina que queda en el quinto pino. Estos de la Seguridad Social te hacen dar más vueltas que una peonza

First of all you have to go to God-knows-where to find the form next you get sent somewhere else to get it stamped. And then you have to hand it in to some office in the back of beyond. Those guys at the Social Security office have you running around from pillow to port

[paquí = para aquí]

El Ministerio de Fomento utiliza un sistema digital para los concursos: escogen a la empresa a dedo

The Ministry for Public Works uses a Knowledge-based system for tenders: it all depends on who you know

[In Spanish 'digital' can refer to computers, or your fingers; 'escoger a dedo' literally means 'to choose by pointing at' — in other words by favouritism]

Tanto con el rollo de que ya somos europeos y esto sigue pareciendo una república bananera. Le semana pasada mi padre me envió un paquete repleto de jamón de jabugo. Los cabrones de Correos me dieron el cambiazo y me pusieron dos piedras en su lugar

All this guff about how we're Europeans now, but it's still like living in a banana republic. Last week my dad sent me a whole parcel of top-quality ham. The buggers at the Post Office nicked it and put a couple of stones in the parcel instead

Government help

Después de rellenar tropocientos impresos me han denegado la beca. En este país se ve que si no estás mendigando en el metro y vives debajo de un puente el Estado no suelta un duro

I filled in a zillion forms and they've still refused me the grant. In this country if you're not begging at tube stations and sleeping under a bridge the state doesn't give you a penny

Mire, joven, es la tercera vez que vengo a solicitor la ayuda familiar y estoy hasta la mísismima coronilla de chupar cola. Yo no me muevo de aquí hasta que no aflojen la mosca

Look, son, this is the third time I've come to apply for family support, and I'm sick to the back teeth of standing around in queues. I'm not leaving until you cough up some cash

The taxman...

Estuve todo el viernes tratando de llamar a Hacienda. Se ve que para variar y hacer honor a su condición de vagos integrales hicieron puente. ¡Es que viven como reyes los muy cabritos!

I spent all Friday trying to get through to the Tax Office. They've obviously all taken a long weekend to celebrate the fact that they're a load of slackers, just for a change. They've got it really easy, the buggers!

hacer puente

Hacienda me ha metido un puro porque dicen que no he declarado todo lo que he ganado este año. ¡Y qué esperan! ¡Con tanta pregunta y tanta casilla para rellenar uno se hace la picha un lío!

The Tax Office have thrown the book at me because they say I haven't declared all my earnings for this year. What do they expect? With all those questions and boxes to fill in, it's enough to do anyone's head in

...and how to avoid him

He vendido mi piso y me han dado más de la mitad de la guita en negro. Como no la puedo meter en el banco la tengo debajo del colchón

I've sold my flat and they gave me more than half the price in cash. I can't put it in the bank so I've stashed it under the mattress

The dole

Se me olvidó venir a firmar el día que tocaba: 10 meses de antigüedad a tomar por culo

I forgot to come and sign on when I was meant to: 10 months of working my way through the benefit system down the toilet

Grown-up little darlings

Estoy hasta el moño de mi hijo. No sé cuántas veces se ha presentado a las opos para funcionario de prisiones. Lo tengo viviendo en casa y en su vida ha dado palo al agua y encima lo tengo que mantener yo. Y lo más bonito es que el niño está a punto de cumplir 35 tacos

I've had it up to here with my son. I don't know how many times he's sat the exam to become a prison officer. He's still living at home, he hasn't done a stroke of work since the day he was born, and to cap it all I have to support him. And the best of it is that the little chap's about to turn 35

> ## Glossary
>
> **apply (to):** echar los papeles
> **banana republic:** una república bananera
> **government exams:** las opos
> **pay up:** aflojar la mosca
> **penalize (to):** meter un puro a alguien
>
> **queue up (to):** chupar cola
> **regard something with contempt (to):** pasarse algo por el forro (de los cojones)

> ## Did you know...?
>
> 'Realizar oposiciones', or more familiarly 'hacer opos', refers to the act of sitting an exam that qualifies the candidate to become a Spanish 'funcionario'. Preparing yourself for this exam entails a number of years of hard work, day in and day out, studying for many hours. This usually means that the few who can afford to sit it are those graduates who decide to stay in the family home until they finally succeed. Many spend years trying to pass until they eventually give up hope.

Test your rude Spanish

Try and match the Spanish sentence with its accurate English translation.

I. Después de pasarme todo el santo día chupando cola, me dicen que vuelva mañana

a) After spending the whole bloody day filling in forms, I was told I have to come back tomorrow

b) After spending the whole bloody day queueing up, I was told I have to come back tomorrow

c) After spending the whole bloody day queueing up, I was told it was the wrong queue

2.   A la mínima de cambio hacen puente. ¡Y los que tengan que hacer gestiones urgentes que se jodan!

a) Unless you live under a bridge, don't bother applying for benefits. They are not going to give you a penny

b) They really get their backs into the work, and they don't have time for anyone who wants to slack off

c) They'll make a long weekend of it at the drop of a hat, and if you've got business to do you can go and whistle

3. Me he hartado de dar más vueltas que una peonza. No quiero ver una oficina de Hacienda ni en pintura

a) I'm sick of running around from pillar to post. If I never see a tax office again it'll be too soon

b) I hate going round to the tax office. The really need to redecorate the place.

c) I get dizzy trying to fill in my tax form. I'd rather let them do it for me

...rude policing

Now that the Franco years are long gone, if by any misfortune you happen to end up inside in Spain you can rest assured you will be treated with the utmost courtesy, particularly if you are a banker or a businessman. So there has never been a better time to set up an illegal business in Spain. If you are harbouring any such thoughts but are short of cash, consider the following: all you need is a cardboard box, three cups, a pea or little ball (alternatively three cards will do), a few banknotes and some accomplices. For your premises just find yourself some promenade packed with tourists and off you go! Your mates will pretend to be gamblers betting on where they reckon the pea is hiding. They'll keep failing to get it right time after time. When the gullible tourist in question realizes that he can make a quick buck, let him bet and win a couple of times. As the stakes reach sky-high levels you will skilfully hide the pea under the cup he is expecting the least, and proceed to take the shirt off his back. Mind you, competition is fierce.

A few useful phrases in context

Unorthodox methods

Yo siempre digo que hablando se entiende la gente. Vamos a ver, o cantas to' lo que sabes o te molemos a palos

I've always said that a nice chat's the best way for people to get to know each other. If you don't tell us everything you know, we'll beat the living daylights out of you

[to' = todo]

La policía se lo llevó palante y le dieron una tunda de campeonato. Se le han quitao las ganas de ir por ahí dando tirones

The police dragged him off and beat the hell out of him. It's put him off bag-snatching for life

[palante = para adelante; quitao = quitado]

White-collar crime

El consejero delegado se llenó los bolsillos y dejó a su empresa en calzoncillos. Untó al juez de lo lindo y lo absolvieron por falta de pruebas

The chief executive lined his own pockets and left his company without a penny to its name. But he slipped the judge a nice fat bribe and got let off for lack of evidence

Habían montao un chiringuito financiero con el que desplumaban a julays forraos de pasta. Ahora van a pasar una buena temporadita en la sombra, pero la pasta ha volao

They'd set up a financial scam and ripped off these rich mugs. They're going to be in the nick for a while, but the loot's vanished

[montao = montado; forraos = forrados; volao = volado]

pasar una temporada en la sombra

Small-time crooks

Estaba haciéndose un BMW para fardar y llevar a su novia a dar un voltio; pero como el carro tenía más sistemas antirrobo que una caja fuerte, la pasma lo pilló con las manos en la masa

He was nicking a BMW so he could show off by taking his bird for a spin, but the motor had more anti-theft devices than Fort Knox, and the cops caught him red-handed

Iban a dar el golpe del siglo en una joyería. Un soplón se lo largó todo a la poli y pasaron una temporadita entre rejas. Los acaban de soltar y el chivato está cagado de miedo porque se huele que le van a hacer una visita, no precisamente de cortesía
They were going to pull off the job of the century in a jeweller's. This grass went and told the fuzz the whole story, and they got put away for a good long stretch. Now they've just been let out and the stool pigeon's shitting himself because he reckons he's going to be getting a visit, and they won't be bringing him flowers and chocolates

El compinche gritó "¡agua!" desde la esquina y los trileros recogieron los bártulos y salieron por patas
The lookout shouted a warning from the corner, and the card sharps picked up their gear and legged it

Le cayeron 5 años a la sombra por birlar una gallina
They gave him a 5-year stretch in the jug for nicking a chicken

La banda esa de chorizos son más listos que el hambre, siempre acaban dándole esquinazo a la pasma
That gang of crooks are as cunning as hell; they always end up giving the cops the slip

Law and order

Los maderos se liaron a porrazo limpio en el Madrid-Manchester para poner un poco de paz. Acabaron con las furgonas a reventar de hooligans
The cops waded in with their truncheons at the Real Madrid-Man United game to impose a bit of order. In the end the Black Marias were packed to bursting with hooligans

Inside

Durante el tiempo que estuvo en la trena tuvo de compañero de celda a un capo del narco. Se pasaba todo el día haciéndole favores y dejándose hacer alguno que otro...
He spent his time in the nick sharing a cell with a big-time drug-trafficker. He spent the whole time doing him favours, including picking up his soap when he dropped it in the showers...

Jorge es un amigo de lo ajeno sin remedio. Cada vez que entra en un supermercado se tiene que pringar lo primero que encuentra
Jorge's a total klepto. Whenever he goes into a supermarket he nicks the first thing he sees

Glossary

accomplice: un compinche
arrest (to): llevarse para adelante, trincar
bag-snatching: el tirón
beating: una tunda, una paliza
bribe (to): untar, engrasar
card sharps: los triles, los trileros
catch someone red-handed: pillar a alguien con las manos en la masa
confess (to): escupir, cantar, largar, irse de la lengua
crook: un chorizo
delinquent: un quinqui
dodgy dealings: el bisnis
drug trafficker: un narco
fall guy: un julay, un primo
flee (to): salir por patas, abrirse
home: la queo
informer: un soplón

local police: los pitufos
open a file on someone (to): empapelar a alguien.
police: la pasma, los maderos, los picoletos, los guripas
police car: un danone, una lechera
(police) van: la furgona (de la policía)
prison: el trullo, el talego, la trena
put someone in prison (to): enchironar a alguien
spend time in prison (to): pasar una temporada a la sombra
steal (to): agenciarse, birlar, hacerse (as in hacerse un coche)
thief (to be): ser amigo de lo ajeno

Did you know...?

The word 'julay' comes from the Spanish gypsy dialect 'caló'. Its original meaning was 'owner of an inn'. The word acquired its present-day meaning of a naïve person who ends up being the victim of a crime because a 'julay' was so often the target of thieves and rogues.

Test your rude Spanish

Try and match the Spanish sentence with its accurate English translation.

1. El chorizo le robó a plena luz del día
a) The thug mugged him in broad daylight
b) The thug stole a sausage during the day
c) The thug doesn't like to operate in broad daylight

2. Es muy amigo de lo ajeno. Como no tenga más cuidado va a acabar pasando una buena temporada a la sombra
a) If they're not a bit more careful, he and his friends are going to end up spending some time inside
b) He is a real thief. If he's not a bit more careful he'll end up spending some time inside

c) He and his friends are big time crooks. They're inside more often than they are out

3. Se ganan la vida a base de dar el tirón. Pero parece que el bisnis anda algo flojo por la falta de guiris

a) They're not bag-snatching anymore but they've set up a scam to fleece foreigners

b) They make a living pick-pocketing. They're lining their pockets at the moment because the place is swarming with foreigners

c) They make a living bag-snatching. But the business is pretty quiet because there are hardly any foreigners around

...rude relationships

If you have ever seen relatives and friends talking to each other in Spain, you can be forgiven for thinking that the whole business of marriage and procreation, Spanish style, is simply to find someone with whom you can constantly argue. However, you would be very mistaken. What might appear to be an impolite conversation, in which the participants are constantly trying to talk each other down and interrupt, all at an ear-splitting volume, is in fact more likely to be a perfectly amicable exchange. When in Spain, if you want to blend in, try raising your voice a few decibels and making your point as adamantly as you can. You will quickly earn everyone's trust and respect.

A few useful phrases in context

The mother-in-law

Nosotros no tenemos ni pa' pipas y a mi suegra le sale la pasta por las orejas. Encima está un poco majara, y va por ahí regalando el dinero. Estamos deseando que la palme antes de que se lo pula todo

We can hardly make ends meet, while my mother-in-law has got money coming out of her ears. On top of that she's a bit batty and goes around giving the stuff away. We just hope she kicks the bucket before she blows the lot

[pa' = para]

Ya le estás diciendo a tu madre que como no me deje en paz la vamos a meter en un asilo. ¡Es que me tiene que decir hasta cómo tengo que abrocharme los zapatos! ¡Estoy hasta el moño de ese vejestorio metomentodo!

Go and tell your mum that if she doesn't give me a break we'll put her in a home. She even tells me how to tie my shoelaces! I'm sick to death of that bloody old busybody!

Married bliss

Mira, cari, tú ya sabes que yo no soy celosa. Pero tampoco puede ser que todas las noches tengas reunión de trabajo hasta las tantas y te me presentes en casa con unos chupetones impresionantes

Darling, you know I'm not jealous. But it's not on for you to work late every night and then roll in covered in lovebites

Le dijo a su parienta que bajaba un momento a comprar tabaco, y no le volvió a ver el pelo en la vida. La pobre como es un poco corta no cayó en que su marido no fumaba

He told his missus he was just nipping out to buy some fags, and she never saw hide nor hair of him again. She's not exactly a bright spark, so she didn't even remember that her hubby didn't smoke

Estamos endeudados hasta las cejas, no llegamos a final de mes y ahora me dices que te han echado del curro...

We're up to our eyeballs in debt, we're always skint well before the end of the month, and now you're telling me that you've been sacked...

"¿Me hace mucho culo este pantalón, cariño?"
"¡Qué culo ni que leches! ¡Pero si estás más chupá que la pipa de un indio!"
"Do these trousers make my bum look big, darling?"
"Big bum, my arse! You've got about as much meat on you as Mahatma Gandhi!"
[chupá = chupada]

Su mujer está liada con el butanero, lo sabe todo el mundo menos él, y el pobre lleva unos cuernos de ciervo impresionantes

His wife's having an affair with the Calor gas delivery man. Everyone else knows she's cheating on him, but the poor bugger hasn't got a clue what's going on

poner los cuernos

One happy family

Mis viejos me taladran el tarro de mala manera. Como me vuelvan a dar la vara con que arregle mi habitación, me piro de casa y no me ven el pelo ni en pintura

My folks are always on my back. If they keep banging on at me to tidy up my room I'll pack my bags and that'll be the last they see of me

Pedrito, deja de dar el coñazo con la moto, ¡leche! Te dije que si no aprobabas todas, no te iba a comprar ni un puñetero monopatín

Pedrito, stop going on about the motorbike, for Christ's sake! I told you that if you didn't pass everything I wasn't even going to buy you a bloody skateboard!

Como te vuelva a oír otra vez, te voy a poner el culo como un tomate

If you open your mouth again I'm going to tan your backside

Friends

La Pepa es una maruja acabá. No se le puede decir na' porque enseguida va por ahí cascándoselo a to' Dios

Pepa's a total gossip. You can't tell her anything, because she goes off and blabs to everyone

[acabá = acabada; na' = nada; to' = todo]

"A ti y a Pedro se os ve muy acaramelados, ¿no?"
"Solo somos amigos, pero con derecho a roce"

"You and Pedro seem to be pretty lovey-dovey!"
"We're just friends, but that doesn't stop us having the odd shag now and then"

Este Jesús parece el pitufo gruñón: está todo el día de morros

Jesús is grumpier than a pig in a Turkish bath: he is in a permanent sulk

Mira, Mari, últimamente estás de un insoportable que no hay quien te aguante, lo que tendrías que hacer es buscarte un novio y que te quite los calores

Mari, you've been driving everyone up the wall recently. You need to find yourself a boyfriend and get a good shag

Young love

Es un agobio salir con esa pava. Siempre que vamos al cine se apunta su hermana a aguantar la vela y a joder la marrana

It's a pain in the arse going out with that bird. Whenever we go to the cinema her sister tags along too, to keep an eye on us and screw things up

Llevaba dos meses saliendo con ella y en un despiste le hice un bombo. Y como su viejo es tan carca me tocó casarme de penalty

I'd been going out with her for two months when I slipped up and got her up the duff. Her old man's such an old fuddy-duddy that I ended up having to have a shotgun wedding

Mira, cari, tú mismo, o dejas de comerte con los ojos a todas las tías que se te cruzan o corto contigo

Listen up, babe; if you don't stop ogling every bird that goes by I'll dump you

La chati con la que salgo está chapada a la antigua. Dice que o se viste de blanco o ajo y agua: no me va a dejar que le toque ni un pelo

My bird's really old-fashioned. She says she's having a white wedding and I'll just have to like it or lump it; she's not going to let me anywhere near her

Estoy harto de ti, con el rollo de que vas a casa de Juan a ayudarle a hacer los deberes, tú lo que me estás poniendo es una cornamenta como una catedral. Si te conozco como si te hubiera parido, tío

I'm sick of you and all this rubbish about you going over to Juan's to help him with his homework. I know you're cheating on me whenever you get the bloody chance. I've got your number!

¡Que sea la última vez que me das plantón! La próxima me vuelvo con mi ex, que estaba mucho más bueno que tú

That's the last time you stand me up! The next time I'm going back to my ex; he was much hunkier than you!

Give 'em some credit

Mi Marisol es una manitas, no hay enchufe que se le resista. Si es que mi Marisol es mucha Marisol

My Marisol is really handy about the house — she's a real dab hand at changing plugs. My Marisol's a real one in a million

Mi Paco es un santo caído del cielo. Hace unos cocíos que están pa'chuparse los deos

My Paco's a real angel. His stews are just heaven

[cocíos = cocidos; pa' = para; deos = dedos]

Glossary

affair with (to be having an): estar liado con
busybody: un metomentodo
chaperone (to act as): aguantar la vela
dad: el viejo
darling: cari
die (to): palmarla
drive someone mad: poner a alguien de los nervios
former partner: el ex
get someone pregnant (to): hacer un bombo a alguien
gossip: una maruja
hassle (to): dar la vara
hassle (to): taladrar, rayar, dar el coñazo, comer el tarro

leave (to): pirarse
love bite: un chupetón
mess things up (to): joder la marrana
mum: la vieja
old person: un vejestorio
old-fashioned person: un carca, un chapado a la antigua, un carroza
pain (to be a): ser un taladro
shotgun wedding (to have a): casarse de penalty
stand someone up (to): dar plantón a alguien
stupid (to be): ser corto
wife: la parienta

Did you know...?

In Spain it's the 'butanero' (Calor gas man), and not the postman, with whom housewives are traditionally most likely to have a fling. So you will often hear him being referred to in jokes and stories about unfaithful wives. Whereas your postman hardly ever goes further than the main hall of a block of flats, where the letter boxes are located, your butanero on the other hand has to climb all the way up to the flat in order to deliver the orange gas bottles.

Test your rude Spanish

Try and match the Spanish sentence with its accurate English translation.

I. Mi novia es más corta que hecha de encargo. Un día de estos me piro y no me ve el pelo ni en pintura

a) My girlfriend's very stupid. One day I'll just leave and that'll be the last she sees of me

b) My girlfriend's very stupid. She wants to become a painter but she's never seen a brush in her life

c) My girlfriend's very short. I prefer taller girls so I'm going to leave her

2. Mi vieja es un tostón insoportable; se pasa todo el día comiéndome la olla

a) My Mum's a real pain; she's spends all day telling me I have to eat more

b) My Mum's a real cow; she spends all day eating

c) My Mum's a real pain; she spends all day hassling me

3. Cortó con Juan porque le ponía los cuernos con otra

a) She dumped Juan because he was seeing someone else

b) She was very stupid not to realize that Juan was seeing someone else

c) She stabbed Juan because he was seeing someone else

...rude schools

Every self-respecting Spanish 'mamá' would be horrified at the prospect of sending her children to a boarding school. The aspirations of her British counterpart, however, will probably be rather different: to pack the little darlings off as soon as they are able to hold a pencil in their hand. Once they arrive at the educational institution in question, they will learn from their history textbooks that the Spanish Armada was defeated by the brave English fleet back in 1588. A quite different version of events is to be found in Spain, where every Spanish pupil knows for a fact that it was in fact the high seas and storms which destroyed 'la Armada Invencible'. Whatever the truth, the following snapshots of life under the Spanish education system might help you bridge the cultural gap.

A few useful phrases in context

Testing times

Esta profa me tiene manía, coge y la muy guarra me catea otra vez
That teacher's really got it in for me. The bitch has just gone and failed me again

En el último examen la profa se quemó por un tubo. Cayeron las tres preguntas más chungas que nos podían haber tocao
In the last test the teacher went right over the top. The three nastiest questions we could have got all came up
[tocao = tocado]

Había empollao un mogollón, vomité todo lo que sabía en el examen y solo saqué un sufi pelao
I'd studied my arse off and regurgitated all I'd learnt in the exam, and even then I only scraped a pass
[empollao = empollado; pelao = pelado]

No tenía ni pajolera idea y acabé aprobando fusilándole el examen al de delante
I didn't have an effing clue in the test, so I ended up copying the answers from the guy in front

Las mates son un hueso de la hostia. Man cateao todos los exámenes este año
Maths is a real ball-breaker. I've flunked all the tests this year
[cateao = cateado; man = me han]

El profe le pilló la chuleta en medio del examen y le puso un cate directamente
The teacher caught him with a crib sheet in the middle of the exam and flunked him right away

61

Creía que el examen iba a estar chupao y al final man follao en las preguntas de mates

I thought the exam was going to be a piece of cake, but in the end I got screwed by the maths questions

[chupao = chupado; man = me han; follao = follado]

Excellence

El empollón de la clase está que se sale este año. Ha sacado 7 sobres en la primera evaluación

The class swot's really outdoing himself this year. He got 7 'A's in the first lot of tests

Claro, tanto hacerle la pelota al profe y al final le ha puesto un sobre en filo

What do you expect? After all his sucking up to the teacher, he gave him an A in Philosophy

ser el pelota del profe

Naughtiness

Lo más díver de la clase de mates es meterle collejas al gafotas sabelotodo de delante
The best thing about maths is giving old know-it-all four eyes in front a good slap on the back of the neck

Le mangué los cromos de la Liga a Gutiérrez. Se chivó a la profa y ahora me tengo que quedar castigao todas las tardes
I nicked Gutiérrez's football stickers. He dobbed me in to the teacher and now I've got detention every afternoon
[castigao = castigado]

Juanito, es la tercera vez que haces pellas este mes. Y no me vuelvas a venir con la excusa de que tus padres se han divorciado porque es la quinta vez en lo que va de año
Juanito, this is the third time you've skived off this month. And don't give me that rubbish about your parents getting divorced again, because they've already split up five times this year

Pedrito, a que no te atreves a tirarle una tiza al profe. Eres un cobarde, gallina, capitán de las sardinas
Hey, Pedrito, bet you don't dare chuck a piece of chalk at the teacher. Cowardly, cowardly custard!

Hard work...

Este año nos tenemos que leer el Quijote para la clase de lite. Es un tocho de aquí te espero
This year we've got to read Don Quixote in literature. It's longer than the bloody phone book!

Este año voy a tener que hacer codos por un tubo para no repetir curso
I'm going to have to work my arse off if I'm not going to be held back this year

Por mucho que me exprima los sesos, a mí las ecuaciones de segundo grado no me entran en la cabeza
It doesn't matter how much I rack my brains; I still can't get my head round these quadratic equations

...and idleness

Como este año no quiero dar golpe me he cogido tres marías
I couldn't be arsed doing any work this year, so I chose three really doss subjects

No pienso estudiar hasta el último día. Si me apetece a lo mejor me lo empollo todo de un tirón la noche antes del examen
I'm not going to bother studying until the day before. If I can be bothered I might pull an all-nighter before the exam

Parental concerns

Tu educación nos está saliendo por un ojo de la cara. Así que o te pones las pilas y las apruebas todas este año o ya puedes empezar a ganarte las habichuelas como Dios manda

Your education's costing us an arm and a leg. So either get your act together and pass everything this year or start earning a bloody living!

Glossary

A: un sobre
big book: un tocho
C: un sufi
comprehensive school: el insti
crib: una chuleta
dead easy (to be): estar chupado
difficult subject: un hueso
do nothing (to): no dar ni golpe, no dar palo al agua
easy subject: una maría
fail (to): catear
fail: un cate, una calabaza
fun: díver
good at (to be): dársele bien
have it in for (to): tener manía
have no idea (to): no saber ni papa, no tener ni puta idea, no tener NPI
intelligent (to be): ser un coco, ser un empollón

know-it-all: un sabelotodo
literature: la lite
maths: las mates
philosophy: la filo
play truant (to): hacer novillos, hacer pellas
school: el cole
speccy: un gafotas, un cuatro ojos
study hard (to): hacer codos, empollar
suck up to the teacher (to): hacerle la pelota al profe
swot: un empollón
teacher: la seño, el profe
tell on (to): chivarse de
tell-tale: un acusica, un acusón
the teacher's pet (to be): ser el pelota del profe
university: la uni, la facul

Did you know...?

The Spanish colloquial verb 'empollar' and the noun derived from it 'empollón' can be translated as 'to swot up' and 'a swot'. The literal meaning of the verb, however, is 'to incubate'. Presumably the link is to be found in the fact that hard-working schoolchildren sit on their books for as long time as it takes to learn everything in them by heart.

Test your rude Spanish

Try and match the Spanish sentence with its accurate English translation.

I. Estuvo toda la evaluación haciéndole la pelota al profe pero al final acabó cateando el examen

a) He bought a basketball for the teacher thinking that it might help him to pass the exam. But in the end he failed miserably

b) He spent the whole term sucking up to the teacher, and it paid off because he got an A in the exam

c) He spent the whole term sucking up to the teacher, but in the end he failed his exam

2. Me he cogido una maría esta evaluación. Seguro que saco un sobre

a) María and I are studying together this term. I bet you we get an A

b) I've chosen a really easy subject this term. I bet you I get an A

c) María, this term's teacher, has given me an A

3. Pepa está que se sale este año. Ha hecho codos por un tubo y ha aprobado todos los exámenes

a) Pepa has dropped out of school this year. She broke her elbow and couldn't sit her final exams

b) Pepa is doing great this year. She has studied hard and has passed all her exams

c) Pepa is doing great this year. She broke her elbow, so she couldn't go out and studied really hard instead

...rude sex

NB: Readers of a delicate disposition are advised that this section contains material of a crude nature

The website of one of Spain's financial dailies recently hosted a banner advert for an 'adult' website. The banner read something like, "click here and get ready to surf the net using your mouse with your other hand". It should come as no surprise then that on Spanish newsagents' shelves you will find, alongside your Wordsearch and Hello, Spanish magazines that feature photographs of young ladies and handsome men displaying their most private parts and adopting a range of impossible postures. Why bother placing them on the top shelf if they will just have to come down anyway, is the down-to-earth Spanish attitude.

A few useful phrases in context

Arousal

María le tocó el paquete y se quedó impresionada por la firmeza del miembro. La noche prometía
María felt his bulging trouser front and was impressed by the firmness of his tool. A promising night lay ahead

Este va tan salío que ve a un perra en pelotas y se le empalma
He's so bloody randy that the sight of a naked dog is enough to give him a hard-on
[salío = salido]

Cuando voy a la playa en verano me pongo enfermo con tanto tetamen suelto. Siempre que salgo del agua voy to' empalmao
When I go to the beach in the summer I go crazy seeing all those tits all over the place. I've always got a huge stiffy when I get out of the water
[to' = todo; empalmao = empalmado]

DIY

Se había prometido a sí misma que no echaría un polvo hasta que pasase por la sacristía. Y para las emergencias guardaba el consolador en la mesilla de noche
She'd promised herself she wouldn't have a shag until she'd been up the aisle. And for emergencies she had a dildo in the bedside table

Desde que lo dejó su novia se la machaca más que un mono
Since his girlfriend has left him he's had more Sherman tanks than the US Army

A ese, de tanto pelársela le van a salir callos en las manos
If he carries on wanking so much he's going to end up with blisters on his hands

The love that dare not speak its name

Se metió en el cuarto oscuro buscando tema. Antes de que pudiera decir esta boca es mía ya lo habían enculado
He went into the darkroom to look for some action. Before he could even open his mouth someone had taken him up the arse

Adultery

Al llegar a casa y ver en el suelo el sujetatetas de su parienta se le puso morcillona, pero cuando abrió la puerta de la habitación y vio al cartero a punto de hincársela se le pasó la calentura de golpe
When he got home and spotted his wife's bra on the floor he started to get a stiffy, but when he opened the door and saw the postie about to get stuck in he suddenly lost interest

Estaba echando un quiqui de órdago con la Pepi y nos pilló mi mujer. Menos mal que se lo tomó a bien, y acabó apuntándose a la fiesta
I was screwing the arse off Pepi when my wife walked in. Just as well she took it in good heart and ended up getting in on the action

Sex as a commodity

Su parienta no sabía que una vez al mes se cogía un día de fiesta entre semana para echar una canita al aire. Se conocía todos los puticlubs de la ciudad
His missus didn't know that once a month he took the day off to have some fun. He knew every knocking shop in the city

Hace tres meses que no mojo y voy un poco desesperado. Me parece que voy a acabar teniendo que rascarme el bolsillo
It's been three months since I've had my end away. It looks like I'm going to end up having to fork out for it

Me está saliendo caro que mi mujer ya no me ponga. Me estoy dejando una fortuna las en webs porno
Having a wife who doesn't turn me on is bleeding me dry. I'm spending a fortune on porn sites

Teasing

Pepi es una calientapollas, mucho darte coba al principio pero cuando llega la hora de la verdad se raja
Pepi's a real prickteaser. She leads you on at the beginning but when it comes to it she chickens out

Yo en la cama vuelvo loca a mi mujer. Sobre todo cuando al final me la limpio con la colcha
I drive my wife crazy in bed. Especially when I wipe myself clean with the bedspread

volver loco

A mí lo que me pone es que mi novia me la coma en los probadores de una boutique. Y el no va más es cuando la dependienta nos pilla en el ajo

What really turns me on is when my girlfriend gives me a blow-job in the changing room of a clothes shop. And best of all when one of the shop assistants walks in on us

Protection

Ya sé que a ti te gusta hacerlo a pelo, cari, pero prefiero que te pongas una goma, que no está la economía como para que me hagas un churumbel

I know you like riding bareback, babe, but I wish you'd use a rubber. There's no way we can afford a sprog at the moment

Manolo, ponte un chubasquero, hijo, que cuando haces el marcha atrás me dejas tol sofá perdío de leche

Manolo, please wear a johnny. When you whip it out at the last moment you get spunk all over the sofa

[tol = todo el; perdío = perdido]

69

RUDE SEX

Glossary

aroused (to be): ir/estar salido/cachondo/caliente
condom: una goma, un chubasquero
deflower (to): estrenar, dar el estreno a, desvirgar
dirty old man: un viejo verde
easy woman: un putón verbenero, una zorra, una guarra
ejaculate (to): correrse, escurrirse
gay (to be): perder aceite
give oral sex (to): *(to man)* chupársela, mamársela/hacerle una mamada, comérsela; *(to woman)* comérselo
have an erection (to): empalmar, levantársele, empinársele, ponérsele dura
have an orgasm (to): correrse
have sex with (to): tirarse a, cepillarse a, darse un revolcón con, echar un quiqui/polvo/casquete
have unprotected sex (to): hacerlo a pelo
heterosexual: un hetero
homosexual: un marica, una reina
lesbian: una bollera, una camionera, una tortillera

masturbate (to): hacerse una paja; *(men only)* hacese una manola, cascársela, pelársela, machacársela, hacerse una gayola
masturbate a lot (to): matarse a pajas, machacársela como un mono
naked: en pelotas, en bolas, en pelota picada
penetrate (to): clavarla, hincarla, endiñarla
pimp (to): chulear
pimp: un chulo
prostitute (to work as a): hacer las aceras, hacer la calle
rent boy: un chapero
semen: la leche, el pringue, la savia, la lefa
shag pad: un picadero
sodomize (to): encular, dar por el culo, petar el culo
spread one s legs (to): despatarrarse
start to get an erection (to): ponerse morcillona
tease: calientapollas, calientabraguetas
trouser bulge: el paquete, el bulto
turn on (to): poner

Did you know...?

'Capullo' is one of those multipurpose words. In standard Spanish it designates a 'flower bud'. However, because of a perceived physical resemblance, it has also made its way into slang Spanish to refer to the glans penis. In turn, just like the English 'dickhead', 'capullo' can also be used of a stupid person.

Test your rude Spanish

Try and match the Spanish sentence with its accurate English translation.

1. Paso de echar un polvo encima de la mesa porque luego tengo la espalda jodida una semana

a) I don't want to have sex on the table because it's very dusty and I'll be sneezing for a week

b) I don't want to have sex on the table because that'll bugger my back for a whole week

c) I love to have the odd shag on the table at least once a week

2. Se puso un chubasquero y se preparó para meterle marcha al cuerpo

a) He put on his raincoat and left looking for some action

b) He went for a run to cool himself down

c) He put on a condom and got ready for some action

3. Estábamos dándole al ñacañaca y mi marido nos pilló en el ajo

a) We were having a bit of rumpy-pumpy when my husband walked in on us

b) I didn't want to have any rumpy-pumpy because my husband stank of garlic

c) My husband thinks that garlic is an aphrodisiac

...rude shopping

According to R K Narayan, the late Indian writer, if you count the number of thank you's uttered on a London double-decker bus as the conductor checks the tickets, and then halve the total, you can accurately establish the number of passengers on board. Such overuse of the term is simply not found south of the Pyrenees. Indeed, Spaniards are very sparing with their 'gracias', guarding them protectively. Compare these two typical situations in a British and a Spanish bookshop:

Customer:	Thanks *(leaving book on counter)*		**Customer:**	Hola *(leaving book on counter)*
Assistant:	Thank you *(picking it up)*		**Assistant:**	Hola *(picking it up)*
A:	£6.99, thank you		**A:**	10 euros
C:	Thanks *(handing over the money)*		**C:**	– *(handing over the money)*
A:	Thank you *(receiving the money)*		**A:**	– *(receiving the money)*
A:	Thanks *(returning money and book)*		**A:**	– *(returning money and book)*
C:	Thank you, bye!		**C:**	Gracias*, hasta luego

* Optional

It's not that Spanish shop assistants (or customers, for that matter) are fundamentally rude, it's just that during their tender years they were not bombarded with constant reminders to "say the magic word" at every opportunity. Thus the word 'gracias' has not become such a central part of the linguistic furniture of the Spanish language. So, if you are lucky enough to get a 'thank you' from a Spaniard, treasure it and save it for a special occasion.

A few useful sentences in context

Your satisfaction is our aim

Señora, le he dicho mil veces que aquí no regateamos, que esto no es un mercadillo. Si quiere la blusa, tendrá que apoquinar lo que marca la etiqueta. Y si no, humo
Look, madam, I've told you a thousand times that you can't haggle here, this isn't a bazaar! If you want the blouse you'll have to cough up what it says on the label. Otherwise, beat it

73

Una clienta venía a comprarse una sartén; al final, con la labia que tengo, le he enchufado una batería completa. Con la comi que me he sacado me da para ir de juerga todo el fin de semana

A customer came in for a frying pan; but in the end I smooth-talked her into buying a whole set of pots and pans. With my cut I'll have enough to spend the whole weekend out on the town

El traje le iba de puta pena. Estaba embutido como una salchicha y además le hacía chepa. Pero el dependiente se las ingenió para convercerle de le que quedaba clavado

He looked a right state in the suit. He was squeezed in like a sausage, with a great big bulge at the back. But the shop assistant managed to convince him that it fitted like a glove

Rip-off Spain

¡Otra vez usted, señora! Pero ¿no decía que no volvía más a nuestra tienda porque éramos unos careros y que esto era un robo a mano armada?

Oh, it's you again madam! But didn't you say you weren't coming back because we charged the earth and that our prices were daylight robbery?

¡60 euros por unos gayumbos que ni siquiera se pueden lavar a máquina! ¿Pero de qué vais?

60 euros for a pair of pants which you can't even put through the washing machine! You've got to be joking!

Los yanquis pierden el culo por los monigotes de Lladró y las perlas. En esa tienda normalmente les clavan el doble de su precio real. Se lo merecen, por cutres y horteras

The Yanks go crazy for porcelain figurines and artificial pearls. They get charged twice the going rate in that shop, but they deserve it for having such tacky taste

Put it on the plastic

De verdad, cariño, en la factura de la tarjeta de crédito la han tenido que pifiar. El mes pasado solo me compré dos trapitos de nada. Eso sí, la mar de monos

Really, darling, they must have made an error on the credit card bill. Last month I only bought a couple of little outfits. And boy, were they gorgeous!

Mi marido compra con una ligereza que da gusto, y eso que no tenemos ni para pipas en la cuenta. Pero él no se corta, tira de tarjeta

My husband spends our money as if it was going out of fashion, even though we've only got a few pennies in our account. But he doesn't let that stop him, he just bungs it on the credit card

El mes pasado le regalé una Visa Platinum a mi querida. Que si ahora un abriguito de visón, que si un anillito de diamantes, me parece que a lo tonto a lo tonto la muy zorra me está desplumando

Last month I gave my mistress a Visa Platinum card. What with a mink coat here and a diamond ring there, it looks as if the bitch is cleaning me out bit by bit!

Venga, arreando pa' casa. Parezco un burro cargao con tantas bolsas y, además, la tarjeta está que echa humo

Come on, let's hit the road. I'm weighed down like a packhorse with all these bags, and the credit card's been swiped so many times that it's on the verge of disintegrating

[pa' = para; cargao = cargado]

echar humo

Good buys

Mira, me he agenciado un peluco de imitación por cuatro chavos. ¿A que da el pego?
Hey, I got this fake watch for next to nothing. It looks like the real thing!

Me he comprado un BMW último modelo que me ha costado un ojo de la cara. Voy a estar pagando letras hasta que la palme, pero farda un mogollón
I bought the latest model BMW, and it cost me an arm and a leg. I'm going to be paying off the instalments until I kick the bucket, but it looks flash as hell

75

¿Has visto mi chupa de piel nueva? ¿Sabes por cuánto ma salío? Por cinco deos

Have you seen my new leather jacket? Guess how much it cost? Absolutely nothing, it fell off the back of a lorry!

[ma = me ha; salío = salido; deos = dedos]

Paso de comprarme compacts originales. Yo me los pillo tos del Top Manta, que están tiraos y, además, puedo regatear

I'm done with buying original CDs. I buy them from a street trader, they're dirt-cheap and what's more you can haggle.

[tos = todos; tiraos = tirados]

Encounters with one's fellow shoppers

Mira, cacho guarra, este top lo he visto yo antes, pero como ya le has hecho un par de agujeros con las uñas de tanto tirar, lo voy a soltar y te lo puedes meter por donde te quepa

Hey, you slag, I saw that boob tube before you, but now you've scratched it to bits with all your pulling, I'm going to let go of it so you can stick it where it belongs!

Señora, no se cuele que ha llegao la última y nosotras llevamos toda la santa mañana esperando. ¡A hacer cola como está mandao!

Hey, no queue-jumping! You were the last one to arrive and we've all been waiting since the crack of dawn. Get in line like the rest of us!

[llegao = llegado; mandao = mandado]

Spoilt little darlings

Mi hijo es un pijo acabado, le hace ascos a todo lo que no lleva un cocodrilo

My son's a terrible snob: he turns his nose up at anything which doesn't have a designer label

La casa está llena de trastos con todas las consolas de videojuegos de mi niño. Siempre se encapricha con la última pijotada y no para hasta que se la acabamos por comprar

The house is full of junk with all my kids video consoles. He's a sucker for whatever the latest gadget is and doesn't let up until we end up buying it for him

Glossary

bargain: una ganga
bra: un sujetatetas
garment: un trapito
gorgeous: mono
illegal street trade: el Top Manta
jump the queue (to): colarse
make a lot of money (to): hacer el agosto
naff: cursi
outfit: un modelito
pay (to): apoquinar
pricey: carero
rip-off (to be a): ser un robo a mano armada, ser un timo
rip off (to): timar, tangar
rip-off: un timo

run up a credit card bill (to): tirar de plástico/tarjeta
smooth-talker (to be a): tener labia
snob: un pijo
spend all sb's money (to): desplumar
swimming trunks: taparrabos
tacky: hortera
underpants: unos gayumbos
very cheap (to be): ser un regalo, estar tirado, costar cuatro chavos
very expensive (to be): costar un ojo de la cara/un riñón/un cojón de mico/un huevo/ un huevo y la yema de otro
watch: un peluco

Did you know...?

With the advent of CD burners, street vendors all over Spain have spotted a new niche in the market. They have added pirate music CDs to their product range of handbags, scarves, toys, etc for passers-by to purchase. A new term has been coined recently to describe the phenomenon: 'Top Manta'. This is a combination of 'Los 40 Principales' (the Spanish equivalent of 'The Top 40') and the more mundane 'manta' (blanket), on which the street vendors display their merchandise, and into which they can roll all their goodies if they need to make a quick exit when the police turn up.

Test your rude Spanish

Try and match the Spanish sentence with its accurate English translation.

1. Se compró un peluco nuevo
a) She bought a new wig
b) She bought a new watch
c) She bought a new skirt

2. Lleva un modelito que le habrá costado un ojo de la cara
a) She's wearing an expensive outfit
b) She's got her eye on an expensive outfit
c) She's seeing a model with beautiful eyes

3. A finales de mes siempre tira de plástico

a) Towards the end of the month he throws his credit card away
b) Towards the end of the month he runs out of credit
c) Towards the end of the month he uses his credit card a lot

...rude work

If you happen to see your Spanish boss accompanied by someone wearing a frock coat and top hat, you might think that he has some rather weird acquaintances. But far from it. If you look at this man's briefcase, you are very likely to see the words 'cobrador del frac' in white letters against a black background. The man in question is a 'debt collector' and your boss or your company must owe a large enough amount of money for a creditor to have engaged his services. Hoping that sheer embarrassment will make them cough up, Spanish debt collecting agencies will often dispatch a bizarrely dressed employee to follow the debtor; costumes could include a pink panther, a bagpiper or a bullfighter – the more bizarre the better.

If you happen to be working for a more respectable firm, here is a tip for you: do not walk around the office with your shoes off, no matter how badly your feet need some relief. It will be widely frowned upon as not following office etiquette. You certainly won't see anyone else shoeless, let alone barefoot; except maybe for that chap waiting in reception clad in a Native American outfit, which tells you it's time to find yourself a new, more solvent, employer.

A few useful phrases in context

Get a job!

He encontrado curro. Me han hecho un contrato basura, me pagan la mitad del sueldo mínimo y tengo que hacer más horas que un reloj sin ver un duro de más. Pero no me quejo, no me vayan a dar puerta

I've found a job. They've given me a temporary contract which isn't worth the paper it's written on, the pay is half the minimum wage, and I have to work my arse off without getting a penny extra. But I don't grouse about it, otherwise I'd get the sack

Mi objetivo en la vida es vivir del cuento. Currar pocas horas, no dar ni golpe y cobrar una pasta gansa

I want to find myself a really cushy number. Short hours, no need to lift a finger all day, and a nice fat pay cheque at the end of the month

More money... or not

Le he pedido más pasta al jefe y me ha dicho que lo tengo más negro que el sobaco de un grillo

I asked the boss for some more cash and he told me I had more chance of winning the lottery

Comprendo que la empresa esté pasando por un momento chungo, pero yo no curro por amor al arte, tengo cinco bocas que alimentar
I know the company's going through a sticky patch, but I don't work just for the love of it, I've got five mouths to feed

Con la subida de mierda que me han dado este año no me llega ni para pipas
The shitty pay rise they've given me this year is barely enough to buy a packet of crisps

Todo el año sudando la gota gorda y te lo agradecen con dos palmaditas en la espalda y un lote de Navidad de mala muerte
You spend the whole year slaving away, and all the thanks you get is a pat on the back and a crappy Christmas hamper

Ambition

Es un trepa nato, por un ascenso vendería hasta a su madre
He's really pushy. He'd sell his own mother if he thought it would get him promoted

Lleva menos de un año en la empresa y ya la han puesto de secretaria de dirección. ¡Si yo me bajara las bragas con tanta facilidad, también subiría como la espuma, no te jode!
She's been with the company for less than a year and she's already been made PA to the MD. Christ, if I spread my legs as often as she does I'd shoot up the ladder too!

Working conditions

El dire es un rata acabado. No nos deja poner el aire acondicionado hasta que no empezamos a sudar la gota gorda. No sabe qué hacer para ahorrarle dinero a la empresa
The boss is a stingy git. He won't let us turn the air conditioning on until we're sweating like pigs. Anything to save the company some cash

El sistema informático de la oficina es una birria, cada dos por tres se cuelga y, hale, todo el mundo a reiniciar los ordenatas
The computer system in the office is a load of crap. It crashes every five minutes and then we all have to restart our bloody computers again

En el curro voy de puto culo estos meses. Y encima se atreven a decirme que voy a ritmo de tortuga y que le estoy costando pasta a la empresa
I've been working my arse off for the last four months. And they have the nerve to tell me I'm going at a snail's pace and costing the company dough

Ya se ha vuelto a joder el fluorescente. Si es que tenemos una instalación del año de Mariacastaña. Anda, llama al chispas pa' que lo arregle
The fluorescent tube's blown again. No wonder, given our prehistoric wiring. Go on, call the sparks to fix it
[*pa' = para*]

Redundancies

Media vida dejándome los cuernos por la empresa y así me lo pagan: poniéndome en la puta calle

I spend half my life slogging my guts out for the company and this is how they reward me: by slinging me out on my arse!

Han chapao la fábrica pa' llevársela a un país del Este y nos han dao a tos la patá en el culo

They've shut the factory down, shipped it all off to somewhere in Eastern Europe, and given us all the push

[chapao = chapado; pa' = para; dao = dado; tos = todos; patá = patada]

Demanding bosses

El jefe es un negrero de la hostia. Se tira tol día paseando por la oficina, látigo en mano, dando por culo a to' Dios

The boss is a right bloody slavedriver. He spends the whole day wandering around the office, whip in hand, making everyone's life a real nightmare

[tol = todo el; to' = todo]

Hey, tío, hoy al jefe ni le rechistes, eh, porque está que saca humo

Hey, man, don't even think about giving the boss any lip today. He's already got smoke coming out of his ears

Móntatelo como quieras, Julián, pero mañana te quiero fichando a las 8 en punto. Y no me vengas otra vez con el cuento de que a tu suegra le ha dado un patatús

I don't give a damn what you do, Julián, I just want you clocking on at 8 o'clock on the dot tomorrow. And don't give me any more of that crap about how your mother-in-law's just taken a funny turn

Mira, Rosa, a ver si lo entiendes de una vez, aquí se viene a dar el callo, si quieres pintarte las uñas y leer el Hola lo haces en tu tiempo libre, ¿de acuerdo?

Look, Rosa, let's see if you can get the message once and for all, you're here to get your head down and do some bloody work. If you want to paint your nails and read Hello magazine you can do it on your own time, okay?

Me he vuelto a sobar esta mañana y el dire me ha cantao las cuarenta

I slept in again this morning, and the boss gave me a right bollocking

[cantao = cantado]

El jefe tiene mucha mala baba. Cuando haces una cagada se pone a gritar como un condenado

The boss is a real bad-tempered git. If you mess up he starts screaming the place down

"A ver si trasladan al jefe al quinto pino y nos lo quitamos de en medio"
"¡No caerá esa breva!"

"Let's hope they transfer the boss to the back of beyond and we get him off our backs"
"We should be so lucky!"

Employees and colleagues

Ese se pasa todo el día tocándose los huevos. Claro, como es el perrito faldero de la jefa, a él le cuelgan todas las medallas y yo acabo comiéndome todos los marrones
He spends the whole day doing bugger-all. Of course, he's the boss's pet, so she gives him all the praise and I end up taking all the flak

Cada día este Manuel le birla algo a la empresa: que si ahora un boli, que si después una grapadora… A este paso el muy cabrón se va acabar montando una papelería
Manuel nicks something from the company every day: a pen here, a stapler there… If he keeps going at this rate the bugger's going to end up opening a stationery shop

La nueva secretaria no sabe hacer la "o" con un canuto; pero como la ha enchufado la jefa, no se le puede decir ni mu
The new secretary couldn't organize a piss-up in a brewery, but as it was the boss who got her the job, you can't argue with a single word she says

estar enchufado

Juanjo es un vago integral. Aquí solo viene a calentar la silla. El pobre tiene una enfermedad grave, sufre alergia al trabajo
Juanjo is lazy as hell. He does absolutely bugger-all. The poor sod's got a serious illness: he's allergic to work!

Es un pasota acabado, todo lo que le dice el jefe él se lo pasa por el forro de los cojones. Lo hace adrede para que lo echen y poder pillar una buena indemnización
He's a total slacker. He doesn't give a shit about what the boss says. He's doing it on purpose so that they'll sack him and he can get a decent redundancy package

Pablo se escaquea a la mínima que puede. Como no tenga más cuidado, le van a dar puerta
Pablo spends the whole time skiving. If he isn't more careful he's going to get the sack

Se tira todo el día haciéndole la rosca al jefe. A todo le dice amén
She spends the whole time sucking up to the boss. She just agrees with everything he says

The delights of retirement (or get a life!)

Toda la puta vida currando como un negro y me queda una mierda de jubilación
I spend my whole fucking life working like a slave, and at the end of it my pension is bloody peanuts

---

Glossary

angry (to be): sacar humo
boss: el mandamás
close down (a business) (to): chapar (un negocio)
cock-up: una cagada, una metedura de pata
computer: un ordenata
favourite un perrito faldero
fire (to): poner de patitas en la calle, dar la patada en el culo, dar puerta
hassle (to): dar por (el) culo a
job: un curro
managing director: el dire
money: la pasta, la guita
oversleep (to): sobarse, quedarse sobado
praise someone (to): ponerle medallas a alguien

skive (to): escaquearse
slacker: un pasota
social climber: un trepa
steal (to): birlar
stingy person: un rata
suck up to someone (to): hacerle la rosca a alguien
tyrant: un negrero
useless (to be): no saber hacer la "o" con un canuto
work (to): currar
work: el curro
work hard (to): dar el callo, dejarse los cuernos / la piel, currar como un negro/condenado, sudar la gota gorda
worker: un currante, un currito
workshy (to be): tener alergia al trabajo

Did you know...?

The Spanish word 'enchufe' is confusing enough in standard Spanish as it can mean both 'plug' and 'socket'. However, it also has a slang meaning: in an office context it is colloquially used in expressions like 'tiene enchufe' or 'es un enchufado' which imply that the person in question has got a job simply through connections. The image conveyed is that you are plugged into the position, without having lifted a finger yourself.

Test your rude Spanish

Try and match the Spanish sentence with its accurate English translation.

I. La jefa le cantó las cuarenta por haberse sobado

a) The boss gave him a bollocking for pinching her bottom

b) The boss made forty employees redundant

c) The boss gave him a bollocking for oversleeping

2. Le dieron puerta por no saber hacer la "o" con un canuto

a) He was fired because they caught him smoking dope

b) He was fired because he is useless

c) He was smoking dope just outside the main door

3. José hace más horas que un reloj y encima con lo que cobra no le llega ni para pipas

a) José works very long hours and with his salary he can't even afford a bag of crisps

b) José works very long hours but enjoys the odd break to have a bag of sunflower seeds

c) José works very long hours so that with the extra money he might get he will be able to afford an expensive watch

Rude Spanish humour

H ere is a selection of jokes and riddles designed to help you test your knowledge of Spanish slang and, hopefully, tickle your funny bone in the process. Most of them have either a linguistic or a cultural interest. Some will play on the different meanings of a given word, others on perceived Spanish prejudices. Some might not be hilarously funny, particulary when they have been explained, but they still provide an overview of Spanish humour, or the lack of it.

We have translated all the jokes and riddles into English to help the reader, but the crucial bits are often untranslatable as they usually involve some wordplay that cannot be conveyed in English. Explanations of puns and wordplay are therefore given after the translation. The reader is encouraged to try and work out the jokes in Spanish before they resort to the translations and explanations.

Lepe jokes

Lepe, a small town of less than 20,000 people near Huelva in Andalusia, is to the rest of Spain what the Irish are to the British — a source for an endless number of jokes about human stupidity and clumsiness. But far from feeling offended by these unfounded prejudices, most people from Lepe will agree that these popular jokes have actually helped the local economy by putting their town on the map.

– *¿Por qué no hay heroinómanos en Lepe?*
– *Porque no les entra el caballo en la jeringuilla.*

> "Why are there no heroin addicts in Lepe?"
> "Because they can't get the horse into the syringe."

→ **caballo** = horse; (in slang) = heroin

– *¿Por qué todos los policías de Lepe llevan una inscripción en sus gorras que dice "Los Chichos"?*
– *Porque el alcalde fue a Londres y vio que en las gorras de los policías ingleses ponía "Police".*

> "Why do the police in Lepe have "Los Chichos" written on their hats?"
> "Because the mayor went to London and saw that in England their hats said "Police"."

→ **Los Chichos** is the name of a Spanish band.

– *¿Cómo se sabe en un campeonato de ajedrez que un jugador es de Lepe?*
– *Porque es el único que baraja las fichas.*

> "In a chess competition, how do you know if a player is from Lepe?"
> "Because he's the only one who shuffles the pieces."

Why do people from Lepe fan themselves with saws?

¿Por qué los leperos se abanican con serruchos?

Porque les han dicho que el aire de la sierra es muy bueno.

Because they've been told that mountain air is healthy.

→ **la sierra** = a) the mountains; b) the saw

Está el alcalde de Lepe dictándole una orden al secretario:
– *Convócame una reunión para el viernes.*
– *Señor alcalde -le replica el secretario – ¿Viernes es con "v" o con "b"?*
– *Aplázala para el lunes.*

> The mayor is dictating some instructions to his secretary.
> "Call a meeting for Friday."
> "Mayor, replies the secretary, 'does 'Friday' have one 'f' or two?"
> "Put the meeting off until Monday."

Iban dos leperos hablando por la calle y uno le dice al otro:
– *Mira esa vieja qué bigotes tiene.*
– *Oye, que esa vieja es mi madre.*
– *Sí, precisamente te iba a decir lo bien que le sientan.*

> Two guys from Lepe are walking down the street chatting, and one says to the other,
> "Check out the moustache on that old woman."
> "Watch it, that old woman's my mother!"
> "I know, I was just going to say how well it suits her."

En Lepe han muerto cuatro personas: dos en un asesinato y otras dos en la reconstrucción de los hechos.

> *In Lepe four people have been killed: two in a murder and two more during the reconstruction.*

Spanish regions

Esto son tres curas, un inglés, un francés y un catalán, hablando de cómo reparten las limosnas en sus iglesias:

Inglés: *Pues nosotros hacemos un círculo y tiramos las monedas al aire: las que caen dentro son para Dios y las que caen fuera para la iglesia.*

Francés: *Pues nosotros hacemos una raya en el suelo y tiramos las monedas al aire: las que caen a la derecha son para Dios y las que caen a la izquierda para la iglesia.*

Catalán: *Pues nosotros tiramos las monedas al aire: las que coja Dios son para él y las que caigan al suelo para la iglesia.*

> *Three priests, an Englishman, a Frenchman and a Catalan, are talking about how they divide up the alms in their churches:*
>
> *Englishman: Well, we draw a circle and throw the coins into the air: those that fall inside are for God and those that fall outside are for the Church.*
>
> *Frenchman: We draw a line on the ground and throw the coins into the air: those that fall to the right are for God and those that fall to the left are for the Church.*
>
> *Catalan: Well, we throw the coins up in the air: what God catches he can keep, and those that fall to the ground are for the Church.*

Esto son dos compañeros de clase vascos:

– Oye, Patxi, ¿y a ti qué te daba el segundo ejercicio?

– Me daba infinito.

– Aibalaostia, ¿sólo?

> *Two Basque schoolboys are talking:*
>
> *"Hey, Patxi, what did you get for the second question?"*
>
> *"Infinity."*
>
> *"Christ, is that all?"*

> → **Aibalaostia** = **Ahí va la hostia** is a typical Basque Country expression (though used elsewhere in Spain); it could be literally translated as 'there goes the host' but effectively means 'blimey!' or 'Christ!'

What's the difference between a Basque and a Catalan if they both go bald with age?

¿Qué diferencia hay entre un vasco que con la edad se queda calvo, y un catalán al que le sucede lo mismo?

Que el vasco se compra una txapela y el catalán vende el peine.

The Basque buys a beret, and the Catalan sells his comb.

→ Note that 'tx' is the Basque spelling for Spanish 'ch'

Jaimito jokes

Jaimito is a stereotypical naughty schoolboy whose puns on language, a mixture of naïvety and naughtiness, embarrass both his parents and teachers. The character has become part of the popular imagery of the Spanish-speaking world.

En la clase de castellano la maestra le pregunta a Jaimito:
– Jaimito, en la oración: María está disfrutando, ¿dónde está el sujeto?
– Muy fácil, seño, ¡pues encima de ella!

> In Spanish class, the teacher asks Jaimito, 'Jaimito, in the sentence 'María is enjoying herself', where is the subject?
> "That's easy, Miss. On top of María!"

– Mamá, cuando terminas de hacer el amor con papá, ¿le das las gracias? – pregunta Jaimito.
– Pues… no, no siempre…
– Entonces ¿qué es educación sexual?

> "Mum, when you've made love with dad, do you say thank you?" asks Jaimito.
> "Well … no, not always."
> "So, what is 'sexual education', then?"

→ **educación** = a) education; b) good manners

88

Comparisons

The kind of jokes Spaniards enjoy most are probably those which involve farfetched metaphors or outright exaggerations. Chiquito de la Calzada, the Andalusian stand-up comedian who coined such outlandish expressions as 'la caidita de Roma' (the little Fall of Rome) meaning 'sexual intercourse', is the person responsible for popularizing these jokes in recent years.

Tienes menos detalles que el salpicadero de un Dos Caballos.

> *You've got less features than the dashboard of a 2CV.*
> → **detalle** = a) features; b) considerate touch

Tienes más plumas que una pelea de gallos.

> *You've got more feathers than a cockfight / You're camper than a row of tents.*
> → **tener mucha pluma** = a) to have a lot of feathers; b) (in slang) to be very camp

Eres más feo que el parto de Mick Jagger.

> *You're uglier than Mick Jagger when he was born.*

Es más largo que la infancia de Heidi.

> *It's longer than Heidi's childhood.*
> → **Heidi** was a young girl in a long-running cartoon series.

Foreigners and their funny languages

The comic effect in this type of joke is achieved by using sounds associated with the foreign language (eg Arabic: repetition of 'a', 'l' and (Spanish) 'j'; German: 'en' and (Spanish) 'j'; Chinese: monosyllables and 'ch'; Japanese: monosyllables, 'y' and 't'), together with some prejudices regarding the culture in question. In order to crack it properly you have to try to mimic accurately the relevant foreign accent.

– *¿Cómo se dice aparcar en árabe?*
– *Atalajacalastaca.*

> *"How do you say 'to park' in Arabic?"*
> *"Atalajacalastaca."*
> → **Ata la jaca a la estaca** means 'tie the horse to the stake'

– *¿Cómo se dice 'eyaculación precoz' en japonés?*
– *Yata.*

> *"How do you say 'premature ejaculation' in Japanese?"*
> *"Yata"*
> → **yata** sounds like **ya está** (= that's it!)

– *¿Cómo se dice 'mujer insatisfecha' en japonés?*

– *¿Komokeyata?*

> *"How do you say 'sexually frustrated woman' in Japanese?"*
> *"Komokeyata?"*

> → **komokeyata** sounds like **¿cómo que ya está?** (= what do you mean 'that's it'?)

How do you say 'condom' in Portuguese?

¿Cómo se dice condón en portugués?

Chubasqueiro du pito.

Chubasqueiro du pito.

> → **chubasquero de pito** = 'raincoat for your dick'. **-eiro** and **du** make it sound typically Portuguese

– *¿Cómo se dice 'chino sucio' en chino?*

– *Chin Cham Pu.*

> *"How do you say 'dirty Chinaman' in Chinese?"*
> *"Chin Cham Pu."*

> → **Chin Cham Pu** sounds like **sin champú** (= without shampoo)

– *¿Cómo se dice despeinado en chino?*

– *Chin Pei Ne.*

> *"How do you say 'unkempt' in Chinese?"*
> *"Chin Pei Ne."*

> → **Chin Pei Ne** sounds like **sin peine** (= without a comb)

– *¿Cómo se dice 'autobús' en alemán?*

– *Subanestrujenbajen.*

> *"How do you say 'bus' in German?"*
> *"Subanestrujenbajen."*

> → **suban, estrujen, bajen** means 'get on, squash up, get off'

– *¿Cómo se dice 'llover' en alemán?*
– *Gotascaen.*

> "How do you say 'to rain' in German?"
> "Gotascaen."
>> → **gotas caen** means 'raindrops are falling'. The verb at the end mimics German word order

Un hombre entra en una farmacia:
– *¿Hay ampollas?*
Y responde el dependiente muy amable:
– *Welcome Míster Pollas.*

> A man goes into a chemist:
> "Do you sell ampoules?"
> A very friendly shop assistant replies:
> "Welcome Mr Pollas."
>> → **hay ampollas** sounds like 'I am Pollas'. **Polla** means 'penis'

Sexist jokes

About men

– *¿Por qué los hombres se ponen tan contentos cuando terminan un puzzle en dos meses?*
– *Porque en la caja ponía de tres a cinco años.*

> "Why are men so pleased with themselves when they finish a jigsaw puzzle in two months?"
> "Because on the box it says 'from three to five years'."

– *¿Qué significa 'ayudar en la limpieza de la casa'?*
– *Levantar los pies cuando la mujer pasa la aspiradora.*

> "What does 'helping with the housework' mean?"
> "Lifting your feet so the wife can get by with the hoover."

– *¿Cómo se llama el pellejito inservible que está alrededor del pene?*
– *Hombre.*

> "What do you call the useless piece of skin around the penis?"
> "A man."

– *¿Cómo se llaman los hombres operados de vasectomía?*
– *Sacarinos, porque endulzan pero no engordan.*

> "What do you call men who've had a vasectomy?"

"Saccharine, because they keep you sweet without making you fat."

→ **sacarina** is here given the masculine ending '-o' to sound like a man's name

Why is a man like a rumour?

¿En qué se parece un hombre a un rumor?

En que los dos se corren enseguida.

Because they both get around in no time.

→ **correrse** = a) to get around; b) (in slang) to come

– *¿Por qué los hombres no pueden coger la enfermedad de las vacas locas?*
– *Porque son todos unos cerdos.*

    "Why can't men catch mad cow disease?"
    "Because they're all pigs."

– *¿En qué se parecen los hombres al parchís?*
– *En que se comen una y cuentan veinte.*

    "Why are men like ludo?"
    "Because they take one and count twenty."

→ One of the rules of ludo is that if you take ('**comer**') someone else's counter you can move forward ('**contar**') twenty squares. **Comerse una** in slang means 'to get off with a woman'. **Contar veinte** in this context means 'to claim that you've got off with twenty'.

– *¿Qué es una esposa?*
– *Una mujer que ha pasado muchas Navidades, pero pocas Noches Buenas.*

    "What is a wife?"
    "A woman who's had lots of Christmases but not very many Christmas Eves."

→ **Noche Buena** = Christmas Eve; **pasar una noche buena** means 'to have a good night'

– *¿En qué se parecen los hombres a los cepillos de dientes?*
– *En que sin el mango no sirven para nada.*

> "Why are men like toothbrushes?"
> "Because without the handle they're no use at all."

About women

– *¿En qué se parecen las mujeres a las computadoras?*
– *En que a los tres meses de tener una, aparece otra mucho mejor.*

> "Why are women like computers?"
> "Because three months after you get one there's a much better one available!"

– *¿En qué se parecen las mujeres a las hormigas?*
– *En que les tapas el agujero y se vuelven locas.*

> "Why are women like ants?"
> "Because if you fill their hole they go wild."

Why is a woman like a parachute?

¿Qué tienen en común las mujeres y los paracaídas?

Que si no se abren te la cascas.

Because if they don't open up you crash.

→ **cascársela** = a) (colloquial) to crash; b) (in slang) to masturbate

– *¿Qué diferencia hay entre una puta y una hija de puta?*
– *La puta es la que se acuesta con todos; la hija de puta es la que se acuesta con todos menos contigo.*

> "What's the difference between a whore and a daughter of a whore?"
> "A whore goes to bed with everyone; a daughter of a whore goes to bed with everyone except you."

→ **hija de puta** is the equivalent of "bitch"

Playing charades

These are very popular riddles amongst Spanish youngsters. The punchline sounds like the title of an actual film, but the surreal situation is what creates the comic effect.

– *Se abre el telón y se ve a Kiko diciéndole a sus compañeros 'dejadme chutar el penalty, que meto gol, os lo juro de verdad'. Lo chuta y falla. Se cierra el telón. ¿Cómo se llama la película?*

– *Pa qué juras, Kiko.*

> "The curtain opens, and Kiko is saying to his teammates, 'let me take the penalty, I'll score, I promise.' He takes the penalty and misses. The curtain closes. What's the film called?"
>
> "Why bother promising, Kiko?"

→ **Pa (ra) qué juras, Kiko** sounds like **Parque Jurásico** (the Spanish title of Jurassic Park)

– *Se abre el telón y se ve un cartón de vino tinto Don Simón. Se cierra el telón, ¿Cómo se llama la película?*

– *Es tinto básico.*

> "The curtain opens to reveal a carton of Don Simón red wine. The curtain closes. What's the film called?"
>
> "It's cheap red wine."

→ **es tinto básico** sounds like **Instinto básico** (the Spanish title of Basic Instinct). **Don Simón** is a brand of very cheap wine sold in cartons.

– *Se abre el telón y se ve a un gnomo, sentado a sus anchas en la chepa de un tío, y está tan a gusto que dice: ¡qué guay! ¿Cómo se llama la película?*

– *El duende sobre el tío guay*

> "The curtain opens to reveal a gnome, sitting on this guy's shoulders and he's so happy that he says 'This is cool!' What's the title of the film?"
>
> "The gnome on the cool guy."

→ **El duende sobre el tío guay** sounds like **El puente sobre el río Kwai** (The Spanish title of "Bridge over the River Kwai")

– *Se abre el telón y se ve una rubia rodeada de gitanos. ¿Cómo se llama la película?*

– *Los vigilantes de la paya.*

> "The curtain opens to reveal a blonde surrounded by gypsies. What's the title of the film?"
>
> "The non-gypsy and her guards."

→ **paya** = non-gypsy; **Los vigilantes de la playa** is the Spanish title of "Baywatch" literally, "the lifeguards"

– *Se abre el telón y se ve un saxofón y al lado un cartel en el que se puede leer: Sasofón. ¿Cómo se llama la película?*
– *Mal-con-X*

> "The curtain opens to reveal a saxophone next to a poster which says 'sasophone'. What's the film called?"
> "Wrong: with X"
> → **mal-con-X** sounds like "Malcolm X".

– *Se abre el telón y aparece Claudia Schiffer. Se corre el telón.*

> "The curtain opens and Claudia Schiffer appears. The curtain is drawn."
> → **se corre el telón** means 'the curtain is drawn', but in slang **correrse** means 'to have an orgasm'

Sailor jokes

To crack the following jokes one has to pretend to be the captain of a sailing boat shouting to the rest of the crew.

¡Suban las velas!
Y los de abajo se quedaron a oscuras.

> *Raise the sails!*
> *And the ones down below were left in the dark.*
> → **vela** = a) sail; b) candle

¡Bajen los botes!
Y los de arriba se quedaron sin mermelada.

> *Lower the boats!*
> *And the ones up above were left without jam.*
> → **bote** = a) boat; b) jar

¡Todos al cuarto de máquinas!
Y Máquinas durmió en el pasillo.

> *Everyone to the engine room!*
> *And Máquinas had to sleep in the corridor.*
> → **¡todos al cuarto de máquinas!** = everyone to the engine room!; **¡todos al cuarto de Máquinas!** = everyone to Máquinas' bedroom!

¡Suelten amarras!
Y Marras salió y se los comió a todos.

> *Cast off!*
> *And Marras came out and ate everyone.*
> → **¡suelten amarras!** = cast off!; **¡suelten a Marras!** = let Marras loose!

Fun in the workplace

– ¿Cómo tiene usted la cara de presentarse a esta entrevista de trabajo para informático con cuatro idiomas y dos másters, si no tiene usted ni idea de nada?
– Pues en el anuncio decía 'inútil sin experiencia'.

> "How have you got the nerve to show up for this job interview for a computer engineer who speaks four languages and has two Masters, if you don't have a clue about anything?"
> "In the advert it said 'useless inexperienced person'."

→ In a job advert **inútil sin experiencia** means 'only experienced candidates should apply'.

Dos secretarias que hablando entre ellas dicen:
– Oye, Maru, el jefe viste bien, ¿verdad?
Y la otra le contesta:
– Sí, pero desnuda mejor.

> Two secretaries are chatting: "Hey, Maru, the boss dresses well, doesn't he?"
> The other answers: "Yeah, but he undresses even better."

Why are civil servants all atheists?

¿Sabes por qué los funcionarios son ateos?

Porque no se creen que después haya una vida mejor.

Because they don't believe there is a better life after death.

Football jokes

– ¿Cómo le dicen al estadio del Atlético de Madrid?
– Hospital, porque todos los que van vuelven con puntos.

> "What's Atlético de Madrid's stadium called?"
> "The Hospital, because everyone comes away with stitches."

→ **puntos** = a) stitches; b) points

– *¿En qué se parecen el Barça y un pesebre?*

– *En que los dos tienen muchas figuras, pero ninguna se mueve.*

> "Why are Barcelona like a Nativity scene?"
>
> "Because both have lots of figures, but none of them move."
>
> → **figura** = a) scale model of a character; b) star player

– *Uno del Barça y uno del Madrid salen de marcha una noche. ¿Quién de los dos conduce?*

– *El culé, porque lleva ocho copas de menos.*

> "A Barcelona fan and a Real Madrid fan go out on the town. Which of them drives home?"
>
> "The Barcelona fan, because he's had eight drinks less."
>
> → **copa** = a) drink; b) trophy (an allusion to the fact that Real Madrid have won the Champions League or European Cup nine times, compared to Barcelona's single triumph)

– *¿En qué se parece el Atlético de Madrid a los Teletubbies?*

– *En que los dos salen al campo a hacer el gilipollas.*

> "Why are Atlético de Madrid like the Teletubbies?"
>
> "Because they both go onto the field to make an arse of themselves."

Miscellaneous mirth

Animal hospital

Esto son dos murciélagos, y uno le dice al otro:

– *¿De dónde has sacado tanta sangre?*

– *¿Ves aquel muro de allí?*

– *Sí.*

– *Pues yo no lo vi.*

> There are two bats, and one says to the other:
>
> "Where did you get all that blood from?"
>
> "See that wall over there?"
>
> "Yes"
>
> "Well, I didn't."

Socializing

– *¿Cuál es la diferencia entre follar y hacerse una paja?*

– *Que follando se conoce gente.*

> "What's the difference between shagging and having a wank?"
>
> "When you shag you meet other people."

Football, the monarchy and sex

What's the similarity between the prince and Real Madrid?

¿En qué se parecen el Príncipe y el Real Madrid?

En que los dos se cepillan "alaleti".

Both of them screw 'alaleti'.

→ **A la Leti** = a) **a la Leti(zia)** the Prince's wife; b) **al Atleti** Atlético de Madrid

Crossed lines

Un hombre con mucha prisa entra en bar y le dice al camarero:
– Oiga, por favor, me pone un café solo corto.
Y el camarero le contesta:
– No tengo, se me ha estropeado la cafetera cambio.

> A man in a hurry goes into a café and says to the waiter:
> "Can I please have a small black coffee?"
> The waiter replies, "I haven't got any, my coffee machine's broken down, over and out".

→ **corto** means small, but is also what you say for 'over' in Spanish when talking into a walkie-talkie. **Cambio** means 'over and out'

Bullfighting: the best show ever (or not)

– Tío, desde luego, donde se ponga una buena corrida, que se quite el fútbol.
– ¡Toma, y los toros!

> "For me, if there's a good bullfight on, I can't be bothered watching the football."
> "Yeah, or the bulls!"

→ **corrida** = a) bullfight; b) (in slang) orgasm

Body language

*S*paniards, a people given to frantic arm-waving in certain situations, also have a rich vocabulary of meaningful gestures, from the sign of the cross still in use mostly by grannies or footballers before a crucial match, to the universal thumbs-up. They also have a number of gestures which, to the uninitiated, would seem a bit more obscure. Here is a selection of them. To become a convincing gesturer, practise in front of a mirror is highly advisable before you decide to share them with your Spanish friends.

I. To be scared

If you want to convey the idea that you are scared or that something has frightened the wits out of you, take your thumb and your index finger up to your neck, and place them on either side of your throat. This gesture can either be made on its own or accompanied by the expression 'tenerlos por corbata', where '-los' stands for testicles: ie 'to have your testicles as a tie'. A possible explanation for this colourful expression is that when a man gets scared his scrotum tightens up, lifting his testicles. If one gets really scared, with a bit of imagination and a measure of typical Spanish exaggeration, his testicles could move all the way up to his throat!

2. To be broke

Although at first glance this expression might seem terribly rude, make no mistake. It has nothing to do with our V-sign. Its spoken counterpart would be 'estar a dos velas' (to be left with two candles). Some suggest that its origin dates back to the times when the croupier in a casino had two candles to shed light on the game. When he ran out of money, all he had left were the two candles. The full gesture is achieved by moving both fingers up and down on either side of your nose. Incidentally, notice than when Spaniards hold two fingers up away from their nose, no offence is intended: they are simply indicating the number 2.

3. Tough!

This is the non-verbal equivalent of 'tough!' or 'serves you bloody right!'. It could be accompanied by expressions such as '¡toma ya!' or '¡te jodes!'. Bend your arm at the elbow and move it backwards and forwards horizontally. You can either extend the arm almost fully or go for a more subtle shorter span. Either way, it is still a pretty offensive gesture.

4. What a cheek!

'Qué cara' or even 'qué cara más dura' (literally 'what a hard face') can be used together with this gesture. To achieve the full effect, you need to tap the palm of your hand against your cheek and put on the appropriate expression of disapproval.

5. Blimey!

This is a versatile gesture that can be used in a number of contexts. Generally, the most common would be when you are trying to show surprise or disbelief, for instance, as a sympathetic reaction to someone's bad news. Its spoken counterpart would be something like 'no veas' (blimey!). Hold the palm of your hand in front of you fully extended and shake it up and down.

6. It's heaving!

If you want to convey the idea that a place is packed with people, you can use the following gesture: put your hands in front of you, palm up, and bring the tips of your fingers together repeatedly. You can accompany the gesture with an expression such as '¡la plaza estaba abarrotada!' (the bullring was packed!).

How to swear in Spanish

By Dr Carmen Arnáiz
University of the West of England, Bristol

The stereotype of the fiery and passionate Spaniard becomes especially true when they use more colourful language to communicate. When they encounter Spanish speakers, British people may be taken aback by the fact that Spaniards do not follow 'normal' rules of conversation. They insist on shouting at each other all the time, talk nineteen to the dozen and constantly interrupt each other. At least, that is the image that they – the British – hold long before they begin to understand what they – the Spanish – are actually trying to say to each other!

Spaniards swear more than Brits, and moreover there is less stigma about doing so in public, although under the influence of political correctness, attitudes have begun to change in recent years.

For example, exasperated Spanish parents, particularly those with few manners, may well yell at their child who is acting up (the capital letters in the examples indicate shouting):

> **¡ME TIENES HASTA LAS NARICES! ¿ME OYES? ¡ERES MÁS PE-SADO QUE UNA MOSCA COJONERA Y COMO NO TE ESTÉS QUIETO Y CALLADITO TE VAS A LA CAMA AHORA MISMO!**
>
> *I've had it up to here with you, right? You're being a right pain in the arse and if you don't shut up and behave you're going straight to bed*

or, even stronger

> **¡JODER CON EL NIÑO! ¡DEJA YA DE DAR LA MATRACA QUE ME TIENES HASTA LAS PELOTAS YA! ANDA, VETE POR AHÍ Y DEJA DE DAR EL COÑAZO O TE VAS A LA CAMA ¿EH?**
>
> *You little brat! Stop being such a pain in the arse – you're driving me up the fucking wall. Go away and stop being a bloody pest or you're going to bed, right?*

Of course, a milder alternative to these two would be not to use swearwords – and a lot of parents would prefer an alternative of this kind – but that does not mean that it would be softer in force. It would carry with it some sort of threat:

¡ESTATE QUIETO YA, ¿EH? QUE ME TIENES HASTA EL MOÑO Y COMO SIGAS ASÍ TE VOY A LLEVAR A LA CAMA DE LOS PE-LOS!

> *Stop it now! I've had it up to the back teeth with you and if you carry on like that, I'm going to drag you to bed by the hair!*

Coño and joder

Spanish tends to use swearwords and insults not only aggressively, but also as a means of expressing feelings. But even in a country like Spain, where the use of taboo expressions is widespread, this type of vocabulary belongs to adult language. Children are still threatened with having their mouths washed out with soap if they dare to use any kind of taboo expression in front of an adult, even if the same adults who are threatening them swear like troopers themselves! This is not to say that children do not swear or use taboo language – they do. If a Spanish soap opera featuring a row between parents and their teenage children were to be realistic, its version for British television audiences would be just a succession of beeps.

Some of the swearwords and taboo words, however, are so widespread in colloquial Spanish that they have become devoid of meaning. People use them in the same way that a British person would use expressions like "ouch" or "oops". Take, for example, two of the most common terms, **coño** and **joder**. If you look them up in a Spanish-English dictionary you will probably find the "c-word" and "f-word" used to translate them, as that is their literal meaning. However, if your dictionary is big enough, you will also see that they are in fact very mild when used in common colloquial expressions, especially at the beginning of a sentence and with rising intonation. An expression like:

¡Coño! ¡qué daño me he hecho!

could only be translated by "ouch, I've hurt myself!". In the same way, **coño** in

¡Coño, si es María!

simply expresses pleasant surprise in the sense of "wow!, it's María!". In both cases, **coño** could be replaced with **joder** without changing the meaning.

Interestingly, if we shift the taboo word to the end of the sentence, say it with falling intonation and more loudly, then the same expression can become a bit more aggressive:

¡Qué daño me he hecho! ¡Coño/Joder!
¡Si es María, coño/joder!

The first example would now imply that the person saying it is annoyed at what has happened and hence could be translated by a swearword in English, although certainly not the "c-word". The translation would be something like "bloody hell! I've hurt myself!". In our second example, the pleasant surprise is now unpleasant and annoyance or embarrassment is expressed, as in "shit!, it's Maria!"

Both uses are widespread in Spanish and although the second type is stronger because it is more aggressive, nobody would really bat an eyelid when hearing them.

Three Gs - gender, geography and God

Another interesting characteristic of Spanish swearing is that there is very little class difference amongst its users. The differences have more to do with generation, geography and God (religious education) than class. In the same way, there is very little difference as regards gender.

Spanish women use this kind of language as often as men, and in the same contexts, without any social connotations attached to it, especially in contemporary Spain. It is true, however, that 20 or 30 years ago, when women were mainly considered as mothers and housewives, it was almost unthinkable for a woman to swear.

This explains why some Spanish swearing is gender-specific. While a man would express that he is very fed up by referring to his testicles:

¡Estoy hasta los cojones/las bolas!

a woman would typically refer to her hair bun:

¡Estoy hasta el moño!

and both sexes could refer to their noses in a more euphemistic phrase:

¡Estoy hasta las narices!

Interestingly, the female version with **moño** has evolved into the very similar-sounding but much stronger phrase:

¡Estoy hasta el coño!

and, mirroring the male version, there is the new feminist expression, which has a slightly humorous feel to it:

¡Estoy hasta los ovarios!

Women do, however, also commonly say **¡estoy hasta los cojones/las bolas!**, even though they do not have any themselves!

The other difference in terms of using swearwords and taboo language is geographical. People from Andalusia tend to swear more often than people from other regions, and because of their strong religious beliefs, they favour sexual terms rather than blasphemies. In other regions where religious feeling is less strong (for example, the Basque country), you are more likely to hear blasphemous expressions:

¡Hostias! ¡Qué daño me he hecho!

¡Hostias, si es María!

(**hostia** being the Catholic communion wafer)

Again, the translation of these phrases would be exactly the same as for **coño** and **joder**, and hence are mild for non-religious people. The different connotations depending on the position in the sentence are also the same.

Animal names in insults

Spaniards often resort to the animal world when they want to insult people. The usual way is simply to use the verb **ser**, in expressions like **es un piojo** (s/he is a nit = s/he is very short), **es un mono** (s/he is a monkey = s/he is really ugly), and **es un loro** (s/he is a parrot = s/he talks too much).

> **Cabra** (goat) is used with **estar** in expressions denoting that someone is mad.
>
> *¡Estás como una cabra, tío!*
>> You're a nutter, mate!
>
> Not to be confused with **cabrón** (originally a 'cuckold') in expressions with **ser** like:
>
> *¡No me seas cabrón, tío!*
>> Don't be a bastard!

Just as in English, the pig family is used to express dirtiness in different ways. Unlike English, however, there are six words that can be used with the same meaning: **cerdo**, **guarro**, **cochino**, **marrano**, **gorrino**, **puerco**), although they do have different uses.

• **Cerdo**, **puerco** and **guarro** are the most generally used. In addition to the general meaning of "needing a wash, dirty" (*¡Eres más guarro que los cerdos!*), you can also use them if somebody has annoyed you:

Mi jefe es un cerdo, no me deja cogerme las vacaciones en agosto
> My boss is a pig, he doesn't let me have my holidays in August

You can also use them in the sense of "pervert". So to a typical Spanish flirtatious comment that a man might say to a woman in the street like **¡qué polvo tienes!**, (literally, "you're a good shag!"), the woman could respond: **¡cerdo!**

• **Cochino**, **marrano** and **gorrino** are normally used when talking to children and are milder. Their most common use is in the sense of "needing a wash" or "being dirty":

¡No seas gorrino y lávate!
> Don't be a pig; wash yourself!

The donkey family supplies another large group of terms: **burro**, **zopenco**, **asno**, **bruto** and **bestia**. **Zopenco** and **asno** are not as commonly used as **burro**, **bestia** and **bruto** but they all generally imply that somebody is not very intelligent:

¡Zopenco!, ¡Que no sabes hacer la "o" con un canuto!
> You ass! You can't even spell your own name!
> [literally, you couldn't write a letter 'o' even with a cylinder (to draw round)]

¡Más asno y rebuzna!
> If he was any more stupid, he'd bray!

• **bruto** is also used to express that somebody is careless or clumsy:

¡Bruto! ¡Que lo vas a romper!
> You ass, you're going to break it!

• **burro** and **bruto** can also denote someone who is coarse:

¡Eres más bruto que un arado!
> You ham-fisted clodhopper!
> [literally, you're clumsier than a plough]

• **bestia** (beast) is a stronger term:

¡Hala! ¡Qué bestia! ¿Has visto cómo nos ha adelantado?
> What an ass! Did you see the way he overtook us?

There are pairs of animals (**gallo/gallina** cock/hen, **zorro/zorra** fox/vixen, **vaca/toro** cow/bull) that have completely different meanings in their feminine and masculine forms, betraying certain sexist Spanish attitudes. The feminine words always denote negative meanings and are used as insults, whilst the masculine forms always carry positive connotations and are rarely used as insults:

• **gallo/gallina**: The masculine means "tough" or "macho", whereas the feminine means "coward". **Gallina** is only used in the feminine, both for men and women. In Spanish, the most commonly bullying formula in the school playground is the rhyming phrase:

¡Cobarde, gallina, capitán de las sardinas!

> *Cowardly, cowardly custard!*
>
> *[Literally, Coward, hen, captain of the sardines!]*

• **zorro/zorra**: The masculine means "sly" or "crafty", the feminine "prostitute, whore" and is therefore only used to refer to women:

¡Esa tía es una zorra!

> *That woman is a slag!*

• **vaca/toro**: both are used to refer to someone's physical appearance. The masculine means "muscular, well built", whereas the feminine means "fat, flabby".

¡Tío, estás como una vaca!

> *You're as fat as a cow, mate!*

Se está poniendo como un toro

> *He's turning into a real muscle-man*

Disabilities in insults

Here is further proof that Spanish is still not a very politically correct language. Spaniards not only use what British people would classify as un-PC language in their daily conversation, they also use it to insult other people.

• **Ciego/cegato** are two politically incorrect words for "blind". **Ciego** is somewhat less offensive than the colloquial **cegato**. They can both be used with **ser** or **estar** in very similar expressions:

¡Estás ciego o qué!/ ¡Eres ciego o qué!

> *Are you blind or what?*

Do not confuse this literal meaning with **¡tío, es que vas ciego!**, which can also be used to describe someone who is drunk.

• **Gafotas** and **cuatro ojos** are used to refer to people who wear glasses and can only be used with **ser**:

¡Cuatro ojos, a ver si miras por dónde vas!

> *Hey, four-eyes, look where you're going!*

¡Oye, gafotas!

> *Hey, speccy!*

• **Bizco** can be used with both **ser** and **estar**. It means "cross-eyed":

¡Bizco de mierda!

> *Bloody cross-eyed idiot!*

• **Anormal**, **subnormal**, **retrasado (mental)**, **imbécil**, **tonto**, **estúpido**, **bobo**, **alelado** and **corto** all mean "stupid". The milder ones are **imbécil**, **tonto**, **estúpido**, **bobo** and **alelado**; the first four of this group being used regularly by children as well as adults. It is as common to hear:

¡Imbécil, que me has hecho daño!
> You idiot, you've hurt me!

in the playground as in the mouth of an adult. **Bobo** and **alelado** are the mildest versions and are slightly old-fashioned:

¡Estás bobo!, ¿o qué? ¡Es que no miras por dónde vas!
> Are you halfwit or what? Look where you're going!

Corto, **anormal**, **subnormal** and **retrasado (mental)**, on the other hand, are rather insulting. **Corto** can be considered a more modern insult than the three others (which have been in the repertoire for years):

¡Que no se hace así, subnormal!
> You don't do it that way, you moron!

¡No seas corto, anda, que así no se hace!
> Don't be thick, that's not how it's done!

In general terms, it can be said that any disability (**sordo** (deaf), **pirado** (mad), **autista** (autistic), etc) lends itself to insults in Spanish, however shocking it may sound to a foreign ear. Moreover, some of these can also be used as terms of endearment, as is the case with **enano** (dwarf), **pelón** (bald), **cabezota** (big head) as well as most of the ones explained in this section.

¡Ven aquí, enano, que te voy a comer a besos!
> Come here, little one, I'm going to kiss you to death!

¡Anda, ven aquí, que eres más cabezota que un burro con anteojeras!
> Come here, you're as pig-headed as a donkey with blinkers!

Sexual terms and bodily functions in insults

As in English, this is a very productive area for swearwords in Spanish. However, where English swearers use "fucking" to emphasize something, the Spaniards use **puto** (which comes from the noun meaning "whore") instead of **jodido**:

¡Este puto coche tiene una avería cada cinco minutos!
> This fucking car breaks down every five minutes!

¡El puto niño, es que no para!
> Bloody kid! He doesn't stop!

or they use other expressions such as **el capullo de**, **el cabrón de**, **el gilipollas de** as emphasizers. Sometimes, however, only the intonation indicates whether it is used as a term of endearment or in order to swear. The difference is whether the stress is on the swearword or not, although sometimes you can also replace

111

it with a diminutive (**cabrón/cabroncete**) to make it clear that no offence is intended:

¡El CABRÓN del niño, es que no para! (insult)
¡El cabrón (or **cabroncete**) **del niño, es que NO para!** (endearment)
¡La capulla/la gilipollas de mi jefa no me deja en paz!
> *My fucking boss will not leave me alone!*

Many of the sexual terms can be emphasized, if used as an insult on their own, by:

Más + insult **+ y no nacer:**

Más gilipollas y no naces
> You couldn't be more of a dickhead if you tried
más putas y no nacen
> They couldn't be bigger slags if they tried

Other common emphasizers (which would be translated by "a real/total...") that can be used with any insult are:

- pedazo de...
- ...de cojones
- ...del carajo
- ...del copón
- ...de mierda
- ...que te cagas
- ...que te mueres

Es un gilipollas (dickhead) *de cojones*
Eres un cabrón (bastard) *de mierda*
Es una puta (whore) *del carajo*
Es un pedazo de mamón (prat)
Eres un mamonazo (prat) *que te cagas*
Eres un cabronazo (prat) *del copón*

A milder option would be **puñetero**, which would not be as strong as the other words, equivalent to "blasted" in English:

¡El puñetero niño, es que no para!
¡Este puñetero coche tiene una avería cada cinco minutos!
¡La puñetera de mi jefa no me deja en paz!

This type of "casual" swearing for emphasis is more common in Spanish than in English, precisely because the terms do not carry the same strength. Including an insult in a greeting, eg "all right, you old bastard?", is more common among young Spanish people than young Brits:

¿Qué pasa, cabrón? ¡Hace años que no nos vemos!
> How are you, you git, haven't seen you for years!

¿Qué tal estás, jodía por culo? ¡Hace meses que no me llamas!
> How are you doing, you old bugger? You haven't rung me for months!

The most common insults using sexual words are **cabrón/a** (bastard), **gilipollas** (dickhead) and **puta** (whore) in the expression **¡ser un/a...!**:

¡Eres un cabrón!
¡Eres una gilipollas!

Mothers – the ultimate insult

The Spaniards, as we have said, are unfazed by swearwords and very rarely feel really insulted, that is, unless you mention their mother. This is the greatest insult that you can utter in Spanish:

¡Hijo de puta!
> Son of a whore!

¡Hijo de la gran puta!
> Son of the big whore!

¡Hijo de perra!
> Son of a bitch!

All of these are roughly equivalent to English "you fucking bastard!" or "you motherfucker!". If you want to mention somebody's family and don't want to start a fight, then refer to their father instead:

¡Me cago en tu padre!
> I shit on your father!

or their ancestors:

¡Me cago en tus muerlos!
> I shit on your forefathers!

This example shows a common construction where there can be different targets for emptying one's bowels (all the examples below are relatively mild):

¡Me cago en la mar (salá)! [the (salty) sea; salá = salada]
¡Me cago en la leche! [milk]
¡Me cago en tó(do)! [everything]

But try using the same expression and change the object to someone's mother:

¡Me cago en tu madre!

and it becomes one of the strongest things you can say in Spanish, so get out of the way, fast! You may get a violent reaction.

Religion in insults

Religion yields some of the strongest possible terms in Spanish. The most controversial words are those that can be considered as blasphemous (**copón** (the chalice which holds the host), **dios** (God), **hostia** (the host)) because some Spanish people can be really offended by them. Some parts of Spanish society remain deeply religious and so some people who would have no problem using any of the words described in the other categories, would never think of uttering a blasphemy.

If we take the phrase **me cago en...**, for example, we saw that **me cago en tu madre** was a very strong expression. However, for religious people, even stronger than this would be **me cago en la hostia**, and absolutely unmentionable would be **me cago en dios**. These terms must be used with the greatest caution. The best advice is to use them only if you are with people who are using such language themselves. However, a euphemistic version of this ultimate blasphemy is provided by **me cago en diez**.

Some colourful idiomatic slang phrases:

¡Que te folle un pez! Get lost! (literally, "go and get shagged by a fish!")

Te jodes como Herodes, a ratos como Pilatos y a veces como los peces Your problem, not mine! (normally abbreviated to **como Pilatos**, **como Herodes** or **como los peces**, the words chosen because they rhyme)

Ajo y agua Your problem, not mine! (literally, "garlic and water", a play on words from *a joderse y a aguantarse*)

Móntate aquí y pedalea Sit and swivel! (said with middle finger raised)

Nos ha jodido mayo con las flores I can't believe it! I'm fed up! (literally, "May has screwed us with flowers")

Me la suda I pass! / I don't give a toss (literally, "It makes my dick sweat")

Sexuality in insults

Much easier to use are expressions that have to do with moral codes, rather than religious belief. Homosexuality is a good example. The most common expressions are **marica**, **maricón**, **maricona** and **reinona** for men and **torti/tortillera** and **bollera** for women.

• **marica**, **maricón**, **maricona** and **reinona**. They all tend to be used as insults, although not necessarily directed to a gay man. **Marica** can also be used in the sense of "coward":

¡No seas marica, tío, y vente con nosotros!
   Don't be a wimp and come with us, mate!

The same could be said with **maricón**, although this one, unless emphasized by **de mierda**, **del copón**, **de la hostia**, etc can be used as a term of endearment:

¿Qué pasa, maricón?
   How are you, mate?

Maricona and **reinona** are used only in the sense of a very camp man:

Ese tío es una maricona/reinona, ¡mira sus gestos!
   That bloke is incredibly camp, look at his body language!

• **Torti/tortillera** and **bollera** are used with females and only as insults. **Torti**, although an insult, is weaker than the other two.

¡Joder! ¿Has visto a esa tía? ¡Vaya bollera!
   Bloody hell!, have you seen that bird! What a dyke!

In a country with a long tradition of Catholicism, anybody perceived as having loose sexual morals is a good target for abuse. The most common terms are **putón verbenero** for females, and **viva la virgen** (literally "long live the virgin") and **mujeriego** for males, all meaning "promiscuous person". Either can be said to be **salido**, making them a randy person. Interestingly, the female expression **putón verbenero** is stronger than its male counterparts **viva la virgen** and **mujeriego**. This is probably because of the role of women in Spanish society. **Viva la virgen** can also be used (for both sexes) to denote somebody who is laid back and does not consider the consequences of his/her acts.

¡No seas putón verbenero y deja de bailar con todo quisqui!
   Don't be such a tart; stop dancing with every single man!

Class and politics in insults

Most of the insults contained in this category are used to denote that somebody is not well brought up and has no manners. They are not only used by the middle classes, the idea being that there is an established norm which the person being insulted does not meet and is hence considered to belong to a substandard group of society.

• **Pijo** and **facha** are the only terms that relate directly to middle-class values. **Pijo** is used when you want to say that somebody is snobbish. **Facha** is more about ideology, advocating old undemocratic values of lack of equality, freedom, etc. It is related to the word "fascism" and encompasses all its values. Because of Spanish contemporary history, this remains a popular insult in today's society.

¡Papá, no seas facha y déjame ir a la disco con mis amigas!

> *Dad, don't be such a fascist and let me go clubbing with my friends!*

Lola es una pija de cojones, ¿has visto cómo va vestida?

> *Lola is such a bloody Sloane, have you seen what she's wearing?*

• **Macarra** is one of the most popular insults in the Spanish language – used for both men and women in the same form – and one that is almost impossible to translate into English. If **pijo** is used to insult middle-class values, **macarra** refers to the opposite of **pijo**: "yobbish", "thuggish", "unfashionable", "ill-mannered" etc. The word is used in different contexts with slightly different shades of meaning. For example, if somebody is speeding or cuts you up, you can shout **¡macarra!**; if somebody is wearing something you don't like you can say **¡vaya macarra!**; if you think that something is unfashionable you can say **¡qué macarrada!** ("that's so last year!"). You can even use it as a term of endearment in its diminutive form **macarrilla**, to mean that although you may think the person is vulgar, you do not find them threatening.

• **Hortera** and **paleto** are very similar in meaning to **macarra** in the sense of unfashionable. **Paleto**, however, when used of a person, has the additional negative connotations of someone being a narrow-minded country bumpkin:

¡Tío, no seas hortera y cámbiate de camisa!

> *Go on mate, change that naff shirt!*

No te cabrees, tío, es que Luisa es una paleta de narices

> *Don't get pissed off, mate, Luisa is bloody narrow-minded*

Race and nationality in insults

This last category is devoted to racist insults, and hence insults that you may not want to use but that you will no doubt hear. Some Spaniards can be very racist towards immigrants. You may find that some of the insults sound a bit strange to British ears, but this is because the immigrants that Spain receives come from different countries to the immigrants in Britain. Spanish has no racist word for Pakistanis or black people but does have a few for Latin Americans and North Africans.

However, it is very easy in Spanish to become racist with any other nationality. You only have to add **de mierda** to the nationality you want to insult:

alemán de mierda
francés de mierda
portugués de mierda
americano de mierda

Spanish has very few slang words for European nationalities. The French, however, merit two. The reason that the French are singled out may be that they invaded Spain in Napoleon's time, have always been a wealthier country, and were in the habit of setting fire to Spanish lorries transporting fruit and vegetables through France. They are referred to as **franchutes** or **gabachos**:

¡Franchute tenías que ser!

(Acting like that) You could only be French!

• **Polaco**, **charnego** and **maketo**: **Polaco** may be a bit misleading to foreign ears. It has nothing to do with Polish people but with the traditional hatred between Catalans and people from Madrid (**madrileños**). Un polaco is what **madrileños** call a Catalan:

¡Los polacos son unos ratas acabados!

Catalans are as stingy as hell!

Charnego is more or less the converse, being used by Catalans to refer to any Spanish speaker living in Catalonia, and not necessarily one from Madrid. **Maketo** is the corresponding term used in the Basque Country.

• **Moro** and **moraco** are used to refer to North African immigrants and, by extension, to any Muslim.

¡Joder, estamos invadidos de moracos!

Bloody hell, there are towelheads all over the place!

Moro can also be said of a sexist man who is very jealous and possessive:

¡Tío, no seas moro y deja que se vaya con sus amigas!

Don't be such a chauvinist, mate; let her go out with her friends!

Sudaca and **peruano** are both used to refer to Latin American immigrants:

¡Joder, estamos invadidos de sudacas!

Bloody hell, there are Latin American immigrants all over the place!

Peruana is also used, but only in the feminine form, to refer to somebody who does a lot of housework (due to the fact that many Peruvian immigrants find work in Spain as housemaids):

Tía, hoy estoy de peruana y no puedo salir

> *I'm doing the housework today and can't go out*

• **Gitano** is a gypsy. Gypsies are the group that probably encounters the most racism in Spain. If used against a non-gypsy, it means an untrustworthy person:

¡No me seas gitano!

> *Don't try and cheat me*

Gitanazo is used for non-gypsy people who are colourfully dressed and wear very big pieces of jewellery (also **horteras** or **macarras**):

¡Menudo gitanazo está hecho!

> *He's a real medallion man!*

Interestingly, **gitanaza** and **gitanona** can also be used to refer to any Spanish woman with a positive meaning, implying great beauty (long black hair and big dark eyes):

¡Elena estaba guapísima!, en plan gitanona

> *Elena was really beautiful, like a gypsy*

Conclusion

There are, of course, more abusive and taboo terms and phrases in the Spanish language. The list is, really, never ending because fashion changes and old terms go out of the language and new ones come in. Here, we have just tried to explain some of the more classic ones — those which have been in the language for decades and that do not depend on fashions for their use. Remember that, however strong they may seem to you if you translate them into English, they may not have the same force in Spanish.

118

How to be rude – a toolkit

Emphasizing how strongly you feel	y	una mierda un coño qué más una leche una caca un pedo	*¡Y una mierda me voy a ir yo a tu casa ahora!* You've got another think coming if you think I'm going to your house now!
Expressing threats/ promises	por	mis muertos cojones mis ovarios éstas mis niños	*¡Ahora lo hago por cojones!* I'll do it now whatever!
Telling someone to go away	irse	a la mierda a paseo al infierno por ahí	*¡Que se vaya a la puta mierda!* S/he can fucking get lost!
	irse a tomar	por culo por saco viento	*¡Anda, vete a tomar por culo y dejame en paz!* Fucking get lost and leave me alone!
	que te den	por culo por saco por ahí morcilla	*Si no quieren venir, ¡que les den por saco!* If they don't want to come, they can bloody well get lost!
Expressing impatience or annoyance	no me to-ques	los cojones las bolas los huevos las narices	*¡No me toques los cojones, que no quiero oír nada más!* For fuck's sake, shut it! I don't want to hear anything else!
Expressing disapproval of authority	manda	cojones huevos leches narices	*¡Manda huevos! ¿Has oído lo que me ha dicho?* I can't bloody believe it! Have you heard what s/he's told me?
Expressing strong impatience or annoyance	estar hasta	los mismísimos los cojones los huevos los ovarios el culo el moño el coño el pelo	*¡Estoy hasta el moño de que me digas lo que tengo que hacer!* I'm bloody fed up of you telling me what to do!

Answers to the Test your Rude Spanish Quizzes

Rude Accommodation
1.c 2.a 3.a

Rude Drinking
1.c 2.a 3.c

Rude Driving
1.b 2.a 3.c

Rude Food
1.b 2.a 3.a

Rude Football
1.c 2.b 3.a

Rude Health
1.c 2.a 3.a

Rude Nationalities
1.c 2.c 3.a

Rude Nightclubbing
1.a 2.a 3.c

Rude Officialdom
1.a 2.c 3.a

Rude Policing
1.a 2.b 3.c

Rude Relationships
1.a 2.c 3.a

Rude Schools
1.c 2.b 3.b

Rude Sex
1.b 2.c 3.a

Rude Shopping
1.b 2.a 3.c

Rude Work
1.c 2.b 3.a